UNWIND!

UNWIND!

7 Principles for a Stress-Free Life

Dr. Michael Olpin
and
Sam Bracken

GRAND
HARBOR
PRESS

Published by Grand Harbor Press

www.brilliancepublishing.com

Amazon, the Amazon logo, and Grand Harbor are trademarks of Amazon.com, Inc., or its affiliates.

ISBN-13: 9781477819593
ISBN-10: 1477819592

Cover design by Faceout Studio, Tim Green
Interior visuals by Faceout Studio, Paul Nielsen

Library of Congress Control Number: 2013954765

Printed in the United States of America

This book is dedicated to all those who desperately need to UNWIND, find peace, be mindful, and gain balance regardless of their circumstances.

And

To my wife Kim and our kids, Beau, Ben, Jake, and Hannah.
—Sam

To my sweet wife, Shanyn, and our very cool kids, Analise, Erica, Adam, and Benjamin.
—Michael

TABLE OF CONTENTS

FOREWORD

by Dr. Daniel Amen

Some stress is good. It's actually crucial to a healthy, energetic life.

I didn't always think so. I used to think my job as a psychiatrist was to eliminate stress, so I learned hypnosis, meditation, biofeedback, and lots of other useful methods for lowering stress.

Then the science started telling us more about stress. In 2011 came the results of a study at Stanford University that had followed 1,548 ten-year-old children *for ninety years*. One of the big conclusions was that lack of anxiety was associated with early death. Apparently, we need some stress in life: The "don't worry, be happy" people die early because they underestimate the risks in their lives and tend to make poor decisions.

So you don't want to get rid of stress entirely. What you want to do is modulate it, restrain it, tone it down. Too little stress in your life is bad, but too much stress will also kill you early. An optimal stress level means you do the right things, but you don't have so much stress that it begins to attack your body.

Too much stress is dangerous. When you have symptoms like headaches and stomachaches; when your gastro-intestinal system is a mess; when you can't sleep; when you're sad and can't shake it; when you begin to avoid the world because you're anxious—it's quite probable that too much stress is the cause.

Too much stress can actually damage your brain and body. Cortisol is known to be a stress hormone, and during phases of fight or flight, it is secreted at high levels. This hormone causes higher blood pressure, lowered immunity, and decreased muscle tissue and bone density; it also kills cells in the hippocampus, the brain's processing center for your memory and emotions, and it increases abdominal fat. Learning how to decrease these dangerous levels of stress hormones is vital to a healthy lifestyle.

Both men and women struggle with too much stress. Women, however, may be more sensitive to its damaging effects. Females have busier brains and stronger empathy, intuition, forethought, and self-control—but with those strengths also come a greater capacity for worry.

So what should you do when you're over-stressed?

The answers are nicely outlined in this book. It provides the best practices I know of for getting on top of stress.

Meditation, for example, has been shown to decrease cortisol levels. I have published studies of my own, showing that meditation not only lowers cortisol but also boosts blood flow to the front of the brain and raises progesterone levels. Progesterone is the brain's natural Valium—it calms and soothes the brain. Stress hormones steal progesterone, and when progesterone is too low, you feel anxious, tense, and nervous—so you might end up self-medicating with alcohol, anti-anxiety pills, or sleeping pills. These things are short-term fixes for a long-term problem; plus they often have more side effects than they're worth.

I'm not a big believer in the "here, take this pill" philosophy of medicine. Still, your doctor is a key resource in helping you with overwhelming stress. Undiagnosed brain injuries can be a hidden source of stresslike symptoms. Other biochemical issues might cause stress.

But for everyday anxieties this book can help you manage your stress. In time, you can work with your family doctor to help wean yourself off your anxiety, high–blood pressure, and other stress-related medications. Managing your stress can also help you learn that you do not need coping aids such as excess food, alcohol, tobacco, and other chemicals to help you feel good.

This book stands out from other books on stress management in one significant way: It takes a "whole-person" approach to stress. It's about optimizing *you*—your body, heart, mind, and soul. It recognizes that any or all of these dimensions of your life can produce anxiety. It's about getting clear on who you are, what's most important to you, and where you really want to go in life.

My friend Dr. Roy Baumeister has always said, "The best way to reduce stress is to stop screwing up." That's what this book is about—and so much more. This book shows you how to take charge of your life, how to make better choices that will prevent stress in the first place. You will also learn how to turn off the stress response, so you can return to feeling good again.

My favorite part of the book is where it talks about creating a mission statement. Such a statement helps clear your brain of who you are and what you are about.

In sum, along with excellent, up-to-date guidance on the skills you need to deal with stress when it happens, this book also teaches you how to avoid getting overwhelmed by stress. I congratulate Dr. Michael Olpin, Sam Bracken, and Franklin Covey on their valuable insights. The stories they tell bring to life their own and many other people's struggles and private victories over debilitating stress.

Enjoy the journey!

Daniel G. Amen, M.D., is a physician, double-board-certified psychiatrist, teacher, and eight-time New York Times *bestselling author.*

Widely regarded as one of the world's foremost experts on brain science, Dr. Amen is the founder of Amen Clinics. His many bestselling books include Change Your Brain, Change Your Body; Making a Good Brain Great; *and* Change Your Brain, Change Your Age. *He has partnered with Franklin Covey in writing* The 5 Choices: Achieving Extraordinary Results in Work and Life.

PART 1

UNWINDING THE STRESS PARADIGM

HOW TO UNDERSTAND STRESS

If things go wrong, don't go with them.

—Roger Babson

It doesn't matter where you are in the world, most people—probably including you, as you are reading this book—are more stressed out than ever.

Most books on stress are about "coping" with stress. Their goal is to help you deal with the symptoms of stress—headache, upset stomach, irritability, lack of sleep, and so forth.

This book gives you up-to-date coping skills, but our goal is much greater than simply helping you cope. We get to the roots of the constant stress you feel. We help you remove from your life the *causes* of overwhelming stress—which is far more valuable than just treating the symptoms.

As Henry David Thoreau said, "There are a thousand hacking at the branches of evil to one who is striking at the root."[1] There are lots of books that hack at the branches of stress; this book strikes at the root, and that's why we wanted to write it.

Too many books stay on the surface of the problem of chronic stress. Even doctors often treat only the symptoms on the surface.

In this book we go beneath the surface to explore why you're tense and anxious, and get to the sources of your stress.

The dictionary defines the term *unwind* this way: "to make or become relaxed." But it includes an additional description that communicates this deeper emphasis on the real cause of stress: "to loose from a coiled condition." Essentially, your chronic habitual thoughts and emotions that tend to lead to chronic stress have to be unwound, changed, and replaced in order to *prevent* stress from happening. You've spent years, perhaps decades, winding up patterns of thinking that unknowingly lead to high stress levels. These can change. You'll also learn the best known ways on the planet to *turn off* the stress response—to relax.

The truth is that most stress comes from the inside out, not from the outside in. It originates in your own mind rather than in the outside world; that's why it's controllable. And you *can* get control of it.

As the authors of this book, we'd like to explain up front that this book is profoundly influenced by the thinking of Dr. Stephen R. Covey, author of *The 7 Habits of Highly Effective People*. In that book, Dr. Covey shows how to solve our problems "from the inside out" instead of waiting for the outside world to solve our problems for us. Dr. Covey's key insight: "The moment you think the problem is outside of you, that thought is the problem." We recognize that stressful things seem to happen to us, but in reality the stress we experience is almost always self-generated.

In his work, Dr. Covey brings to light seven patterns of thinking that are the roots of ineffective living, along with ways to change those thought patterns. In our work, we have found that the same principles underlying the seven habits can be used to overcome chronic stress—which isn't surprising, as they are simply the basic principles of effective living.

Now, who are we, and why are *we* the ones writing this book?

Dr. Michael Olpin is the director of the Stress Relief Center at Weber State University in Ogden, Utah. Michael has made it his life's work to help stressed-out people find peace. He has taught in several universities across the United States and authored a popular textbook on stress—but his most interesting achievement is the Stress Relief Center itself.

Here, anxious college students learn a whole-person approach to changing their lives. They get immediate relief from an array of amazing machines—a chair that enfolds them and massages every limb and joint, inversion tables for hanging upside down, a vertical treadmill that works your legs while you lie flat—all in darkened, womblike rooms aromatic with soothing fragrances and quiet music.

But beyond these mechanical solutions, Michael teaches people how to live mindfully, get control of their lives, become more purposeful and organized, balance priorities, communicate empathically—in short, to master stress "from the inside out." His students often exclaim, "Dr. Olpin changed my life." Michael shares with you his personal insights throughout this book.

Coauthor Sam Bracken is not a practitioner—he's more like a patient. A successful marketing executive and motivational speaker, Sam spent much of his life debilitated by stress. Abused as a child, abandoned, and left to fend for himself in a world of poverty, violence, alcohol, and drugs, Sam found an escape route from all that through college athletics. But his painful past continued to haunt him and fill him with anxiety—add to that a driven personality and you have a recipe for lifelong, high-pressure stress.

It was not until Sam discovered how to change his thought patterns that he began to overcome the anxiety that was draining his life away. Throughout this book, you will hear Sam talk about how, with the help of Michael Olpin and others, he changed his thinking and purged chronic stress from his life.

Although we might not have the traumatic background of a Sam Bracken, many of us still ache with anxiety most of the time. We might not even recognize it as stress, although our heads hurt; our blood pressure is up; and sometimes we'd just like to scream.

Now, stress is far more than just an inconvenience. We pay an enormous price for being stressed out all the time. Here are some of the organizational and social costs:

- The financial costs of stress are staggering—in the United States alone, some estimates run as high as $300 billion per year in lost productivity because of illness, absenteeism, and decreased productivity.[2]
- Worldwide, 30 to 40 percent of employees report their work as "very or extremely stressful."[3]
- Forty percent of job turnover is due to stress.
- Stress is almost twice as likely to cause you to miss thirty days of work in a year than all other illnesses put together.
- Costs of health care for stressed-out workers are nearly 50 percent higher than for low-stress workers.[4]
- People under stress shift to a superficial style of thinking.[5]
- *Britain:* Nearly fourteen million workdays are lost every year due to high stress.[6]
- Stress is a more dangerous risk factor for cancer and heart disease than either smoking or high-cholesterol foods.[7]
- *Europe:* More than half of job absenteeism is due to stress.[8]
- *India:* Half a million professional workers per year become ill from job-related stress.[9]
- *Japan:* Women who report high levels of mental stress are more than twice as likely to die from stroke or heart disease than those with low stress levels.[10]

- *United States:* Double-digit increases in workers' compensation premiums every year as a result of mental stress claims threaten to bankrupt the system in several American states.[11]
- At least six out of ten doctor visits are due to stress.[12]
- Forty million Americans are on anti-depressants, including 25 percent of women between the ages of fifty and sixty-four.[13]
- *Scandinavia:* People suffering from "job strain" have a 25 percent higher chance of developing heart disease.[14]
- *United States:* The average hourly wage is around $21. If ten workers each lose twenty-five days a year due to stress-based illness, the cost to the employer is $42,000—the equivalent of one full worker's yearly wage for no return.

Of course, you know deep down what stress is costing you personally. You can lose income through lowered productivity or absenteeism—you might even become unemployable. You know what stress feels like:

- Bouts of anger or hostility
- Lethargy, fatigue, mental slowness
- Headache, muscle tension, stomach pain, ulcers
- Insomnia, irritability, depression
- Weight gain or loss, eating disorders

People around the world consistently report these symptoms of high levels of stress. Many select more than one symptom:[15]

- Irritability or anger: 42 percent of the population
- Fatigue: 37 percent

7

- Lack of interest in work, motivation, or energy: 35 percent
- Headaches: 32 percent
- Upset stomach: 24 percent
- Changes in appetite: 17 percent
- Lower sex drive: 11 percent

You might have some or all of these symptoms of stress. You might identify with one of these real people:

Chicago: Christine had worked for fifteen years as a university administrator. She had done all kinds of important and not-so-important things. In other words, she had put in her time, developed a network, and learned a lot. So when the dean's job opened up, she applied for it. To her delight, she was offered the job. And that's when the trouble began. She started suffering from insomnia, staying awake every night and worrying about things. She stopped exercising because she couldn't find time to fit everything in. She started putting on weight because she skipped meals in favor of something quick she could swallow on her way to the next meeting. Life was not so delightful anymore.

Tokyo: For Shigeo, an IT consultant, life was pretty complicated. Just making a living was hard. "It's recession here and recession there—all everyone talks about is the economy." He worked all day and then spent hours at night drinking with customers. "It's necessary to keep up the business." Then he won a big contract for his company. Somehow it didn't help; he still felt more than ever like smashing things. So he did. He went to "The Venting Place," an unusual doctor's office where, for 1000 yen, Shigeo could scream and throw dishes against a concrete wall.

Stockholm: Senta was a public health nurse overwhelmed with patients. After being on her feet all day, she went home to her son and daughter and a night's schoolwork. After the children were asleep, she did laundry, washed dishes, and paid bills—with never enough money. Her back hurt and her headache never quite went away. One day she fell far behind on her appointments. Running to catch an elderly diabetic who needed an insulin injection, she arrived just as the old lady's bus was leaving. So she handed the insulin dispenser through a bus window—but it was the wrong bus. Now she was in real trouble.

You might be like Senta, overwhelmed, underpaid, always behind on everything, and with an interminable headache.

Then there's Christine and Shigeo, who finally got what they wanted, yet they're stressed out anyway. Don't people usually feel happy and accomplished when they get what they've been working for? People aren't supposed to be stressed out when good things happen, are they?

The stress response, also known as the fight-or-flight response, is designed to kick in when something awful happens, especially when we are in immediate danger. For example, from Michael Olpin:

> I was riding my bike on a mountain trail near my home. I rode uphill for quite a stretch and was feeling worn out. The trail continued through some trees, and the ascent continued. I was feeling exhausted, barely able to continue. Just as I came around a corner, I heard a rattlesnake with its rattle shaking. Without a second's thought, I at once had a huge burst of energy and flew up the mountain trail about fifty yards. I was exhausted but at the same time very grateful for the immediate burst of speed and power that helped me escape a real threat."

The stress response is obviously extremely useful. In times of real danger, it helps us to amass great strength, focus clearly, and increase speed.

How does it work? When a rattlesnake (or the equivalent) crosses your path, a region of the brain called the hypothalamus dispatches a signal to your pituitary gland. From there, a chemical signal shoots through your blood. The adrenal glands above the kidneys read the signal and pump out hormones that do all these things:

- Heart rate, breathing rate, and oxygen consumption rate all shoot up dramatically.
- Metabolism and blood sugar skyrocket.
- Adrenalin and cortisol hormones are pumped into every cell in your body.
- Sensory awareness goes up while your perception of physical pain goes down.
- Muscles contract more efficiently, especially the running and fighting muscles.
- The blood clots more easily so you won't bleed out from injury while you're fighting or fleeing.
- Cholesterol output increases.
- The immune system slows down.
- Blood tends to shunt away from your extremities and toward your running and fighting muscles.
- The reproductive and digestive systems cease functioning normally.
- Higher-order thinking switches off.
- Body hair stands on end.

Why do all these physiological changes take place? Your brain knows the snake could kill you, so your body pulls out all the stops to keep you alive. The combined effect of these changes is to make you stronger and faster so you can fight or flee more effectively.

And as you plow through the forest at lightning speed, you might not even notice the scratches you'll be getting from tree branches and bushes—something you would certainly notice while working in the garden but that your body ignores for now, thanks to the stress response. What are a few cuts and scrapes compared to a lethal snakebite?

Once the danger passes, the body returns to a state of equilibrium called *homeostasis*.

So short-term stress—called episodic stress—can be a good thing. It's your body's way of keeping you alive in the face of danger. In fact, stress *defined as a challenge* (eustress) can be highly motivational. If your goal is to lose some weight and you spend ten extra minutes in the gym each day—that is, you "stress" your muscles for ten extra minutes—you may find that stress is your best friend, helping you get in shape and become healthier.

STRESSBUSTER

(This is the first "stressbuster"—a quick tip for unwinding from stress-filled days. You'll encounter many stressbusters as you read. A stressbuster is something like a quick fix pill without any side effects. Stressbusters can be done immediately, and they produce immediate stress-reducing results.)

When you're feeling stressed, get up and take a brisk walk for fifteen minutes. Your body wants to flee, so flee! Then come back—your stress will be reduced.

Stress is good—*unless it lasts a long time* or you are pushing the stress button *all the time*. You see, the body wasn't designed to be running away from poisonous snakes for longer than a few minutes or so. Our bodies are not intended to endure the kind of 24/7 stress that Christine, Shigeo, and Senta experience. Momentary stress is natural; chronic stress is not.

Logically, you might think the human body developed to sustain chronic stress. After all, weren't our primitive ancestors under constant stress due to poor food, bad habitations, animal attacks, and so on?

Probably not. The stress response of ancient peoples was not always "on." For example, anthropologists studying the native peoples of sunny southern California before European contact have found that they enjoyed a rich, healthy diet and were able to provide for all their material needs with just a few hours of work a day. Then they relaxed. Starvation was virtually unknown. Some of them lived to be over one hundred years old, without the aid of cholesterol-lowering drugs or blood thinners to ward off heart attacks and strokes. They lived to an old age naturally.[16] No doubt they experienced episodic, occasional stress, but the long-term, slow-burn stress so familiar to us was probably not part of their lives.

This is the body's basic formula for responding to the sudden appearance of a threat (like a poisonous snake):

THE STRESS RESPONSE MODEL

Fight or Flight (30-90 Seconds)

CHRONIC STRESS

Homeostasis

PERCEIVED THREAT

Exhaustion

Recovery

1. A state of homeostasis—riding the mountain bike in a leisurely sort of way along the trail.
2. A powerful burst of energy—a physiological response to an immediate, incoming danger: The snake emerges, its rattle buzzing.
3. Thirty seconds of fleeing or fighting—an extreme burst of speed until you are far enough from the snake that the threat has passed.
4. A gradual return to homeostasis—you continue to ride your bike, but you are noticeably more fatigued than before.

Your body will initiate the stress response when an oncoming car veers into your lane on the highway, or you see a toddler fall into a swimming pool, or a poisonous snake is about to strike. Short-term, episodic stress does no damage to your body,[17] doesn't shorten your life, and doesn't leave you in a state of depression.

But if you're stressed for a long time—living day after day, month after month as if you were constantly avoiding head-on collisions or running away from poisonous snakes—then your body and your brain are going to be in real trouble. In fact, you could be slowly killing yourself.

In 2006, one of Toyota's top engineers dropped dead. He was only forty-five. Japan's Ministry of Health, Labor, and Welfare ruled that his death was caused by stress from overwork: They call it *karoshi*, which means "work death." Increasingly, workers are found dead at their desks (189 in one recent year!)[18] and the government is ordering companies to pay damages to the families of those who are "stressed to death."

In Japanese culture, people are expected to work long hours, and a worker's status often depends on how much time he or she puts in at the office. For many, a typical workweek is ninety hours.

Many work deaths seem to happen with no prior evidence of illness—workers simply drop dead at their desks. But in fact, their bodies have been marinating in cortisol and other stress chemicals for many years. Eventually, the body just quits.[19]

The culture of overwork and overwhelm is not restricted to Japan. Many of us deal with demanding organizational cultures—and many of us demand a great deal of ourselves.

But if your stress switch is always "on," you have a serious problem. Fortunately, it is a problem you can solve.

Assess Your Stress

(Throughout the book we will have you perform short exercises to discover something about the stress in your life and how to get to the root of the stress in your life. Most assessments will require some sort of record keeping to keep track of answers to questions or other responses to the assessment. You might want to keep a notebook handy, a document on your computer, a good note-taking app, or some other technologically savvy way of filling out the assessments.)

Let's find out if you have a problem with chronic stress. The following assessments allow you to look at your own stress levels from several different angles. This way you can get a good picture of your current levels of stress.

1. **After you have been sitting or relaxing for a period of time, find your pulse.**

Count the number of beats for sixty seconds, and record your resting heart rate.

Next, sit in a chair so your back is primarily straight up and down against the backrest of the chair. Place one hand on your stomach with your palm covering your navel. Place the other hand on your chest, somewhere on the upper part of your torso.

While sitting straight up, become very aware of your breath as it naturally goes in and comes back out. As you take several natural breaths, notice which hand moves more—your chest or your stomach hand. Just become aware of the part of your torso that seems to move the most while you inhale and exhale: stomach, chest, or both. Write down the answer.

While sitting, again breathe normally and naturally. This time, count how many natural, effortless breaths you take in a minute. This is called your respiration rate. Each inhalation and exhalation cycle is considered one breath. Record your respiration rate.

As we've mentioned, the stress response is designed to make the body very fast and very powerful immediately. When we are relaxed in homeostasis, we tend to breathe primarily into the lower lungs, and as we do, the diaphragm moves down and the stomach moves out. When we are in the stress response, we recruit more of our upper torso muscles so that our breathing speeds up to pull more oxygen into the lungs more quickly. A person who has chronic stress tends to breathe more quickly and more shallowly in general, whereas a person who is mostly relaxed tends to breathe more deeply and slowly.

The average respiration rate is twelve to sixteen breaths per minute. A faster breathing rate might be an indicator of higher than desired stress levels. A very relaxed healthy person might take as few as four to ten breaths per minute.

Similarly, a stressed person will tend to have a higher resting heart rate than a relaxed person. The heart beats faster to get more oxygen and nutrient-rich blood to the muscles to create more immediate energy. The resting heart rate of a relaxed healthy person is somewhere between about fifty-five to seventy beats per minute. Assuming a healthy heart, the resting heart rate of a stressed person is typically higher than seventy;

in general, the higher the heart rate, the more activated is the stress response.

Consider the last month of your life. On a "stress-o-meter" scale from 0–10, a 0 would mean no stress at all (life is blissful, serene, happy, calm, and flowing). At the other end of the scale, 10 would mean very high stress, intense anxiety, severe depression, or even suicidal thoughts. Realizing that some days are better than others—some of us are emotional roller coasters—what average score would you give yourself on the stress-o-meter scale? Write down your answer.

2. Record symptoms of stress.
As we've said, chronic stress can have serious consequences for your health, so it's a good idea to take a survey of any symptoms of stress you are experiencing.

For each symptom below, write down how often you experience it—from never to almost all day, every day. If you're having a lot of these symptoms frequently, it's a good indicator that you're turning on the stress response more often than you should.

- Headaches
- Fatigue
- Anxiety or worry
- Difficulty falling asleep
- Other sleeping difficulties
- Irritability
- Bouts of anger or hostility
- Boredom
- Eating too much/too little
- Diarrhea, gas, cramps, constipation
- Depression

If you rarely or never experience any of these symptoms, you probably aren't having too much of a problem with chronic activation of the stress response. Fortunately, in this book you are going to learn how to stay that way.

But does the assessment show that you might be experiencing chronic stress? Perhaps you haven't recognized your symptoms as stress related. Or maybe you have just grown to accept these symptoms as a part of life that you can't do much about.

The good news is that the symptoms that accompany chronic stress will slowly but surely disappear as you learn the principles and techniques found in this book!

Tom and Jessica were finally able to qualify for a home loan. Their new home was in a safe part of town with good schools for the kids. But it was an expensive purchase for them; they had to economize every day to make it work, and there was no wiggle room in the budget. They were, as they say, "house poor," having just enough for a monthly payment, but not much left over. Things worked for about six months, and they saw the tight budget as a challenge (that is positive, motivating eustress) that they were willing to meet.

But then two things happened that launched them into slow-burn, chronic distress that seemed to intensify with every new bill that arrived. The first stressor: Their son was diagnosed with early onset diabetes. The second was that Tom's company, suffering from a slowdown in the economy, furloughed all employees one day each week. The doctor visits, insulin shots, and special diet for their son, along with the loss of pay, made it impossible to cover expenses. For a while, they put everything they could on credit cards, but the cards were maxing out, and Tom had started looking—unsuccessfully—for a part-time night job. Intense worry kept them both awake at night. They felt depressed and unable to resolve anything. They found themselves criticizing each other all the time; Jessica was grumpy and Tom responded in the same way. Adding to the stress, they both kept coming down with colds. In short, they had gone from a challenging, good state of stress to a serious state of distress.

Let's explore what was happening to Tom and Jessica. Stress hormones were constantly pumping into their blood streams, and so their bodies were unable to return to homeostasis; it was like fleeing from a poisonous snake *all day and all night, for months and months.* Under this chronic stress, their bodies were literally deteriorating.

Under stress, your body will produce an excessive amount of cortisol (technically called hydrocortisone). This hormone is essential for life and does you much good—in moderate doses. But a continual flood of it weakens your immune system, making you more susceptible to infection. It slows down your bone cell growth, which over time can lead to osteoporosis. It drains potassium from your cells and makes it more difficult for your intestines to absorb calcium. It interrupts normal reproductive functions such as menstruation and the production of estrogen and testosterone. It causes you to retain water and store excess fat.

It also hurts your brain. After about thirty minutes of stress and prolonged exposure to cortisol, the energy supply to the memory center of the brain, the hippocampus, drops by about 25 percent. Eventually, the neurons in the hippocampus begin to die. The result is that under high or prolonged stress, memory and concentration are impaired. You literally don't think as well as you used to. Your thoughts become more superficial, less rational.[20]

We are all familiar with the "brain freeze" syndrome when, under stress, we go blank. We blank out people's names. We garble our words. We seem to lose our minds. These embarrassing things often happen to people in anxious situations, like to politicians in a debate or to business presenters or, famously, to beauty pageant contestants. Research indicates that this "mental shutdown" is a "fairly common response to moments of high stress—like, for instance, being on stage at a nationally televised beauty pageant. In these situations, the brain shuts off the areas involved in creativity and abstract thinking, as a perceived response to a physical threat," even if the threat is not physical.[21] Although you might never get mental paralysis under the stage lights, chronic stress will continually degrade your ability to think straight.

Another major stress hormone, adrenaline, is responsible for your immediate reaction to danger. When Michael heard the rattlesnake, his legs pumped instantly on his bike, and he was off like a gunshot. That was adrenaline, the powerful trigger of the fight-or-flight response.

But a constant flow of adrenaline puts your heart and blood vessels at risk. The hormone causes fatty buildup in the arteries, which left unchecked could develop into atherosclerosis, a precursor of heart attacks and diabetes.

Chronic stress prevents the body's natural functions from ever recuperating and slowly wrecks the body. That's what was happening to Tom and Jessica. Stress was actually making them *sick*. Are those things happening to you? If so, listen to your body. Your body will often register stress before you become conscious of it.

Because the body knows it's in danger.

Following is the first of several "workouts" in this book. Like a physical workout, these workouts are activities that will strengthen your mind and body against the harmful effects of stress. We suggest that you attempt these workouts with some frequency, just as you would return to your physical exercise over and over again. As you do, you'll see dramatic decreases in your stress levels and dramatic increases in your ability to prevent stress. These workouts have been strategically placed, so you can immediately put into practice the principles that you are reading. You may also choose to write down your reflections in a notebook, or type them using a computer, smartphone, or other device.

Go through the workout before you go on with your reading.

WORKOUT: FIGHT OR FLIGHT?

The purpose of this workout is to help you understand the difference between situations that do and those that do not warrant activation of the fight-or-flight response.

Below is a list of the immediate physiological effects of the fight-or-flight response. Consider how each of the responses is designed to help a person survive physical danger:

1. Next to each item in this list, write down at least one reason why the body would respond to a stressful event in that way. Why would these responses make the body immediately stronger and speedier?

   - Increase in heart rate
   - Increase in breathing rate
   - Increased tension in large (fighting and running) muscles
   - Increase in tolerance for pain
   - Increase in blood sugar levels
   - Suppressed immune system
   - Suppressed digestion

2. Clearly, the stress response becomes your best friend when you find yourself in a dangerous situation. The immediate speed and power that come from fight-or-flight activation can save your life. Remember a situation where you or someone you know found yourself where you had no other desire than to stay alive by escaping.

3. Think about how your body reacted in ways that are similar to those listed above with your immediate activation of the stress response.

4. Consider the following situations that people commonly perceive to be stressful. Ask yourself whether the event is one that warrants activation of the stress response in order to escape from it to stay alive.

    - Taking a test
    - Having an argument
    - Arriving late for a class
    - Being chased by a mugger
    - Giving a prepared speech to a crowd of people
    - Sliding down a mountainside while hiking
    - Experiencing rejection when asking someone for a date
    - Getting a bad score on a test
    - Getting ready for an important ball game

How do you explain the fact that you feel stressed in situations where there is no physical danger involved? What can you tell yourself in these situations in order to put the stressful event in perspective and keep your stress response in proportion to the actual risk?

THE GAP BETWEEN
STIMULUS AND RESPONSE

*The greatest weapon against stress is our ability
to choose one thought over another.*

—*William James*

Now we know that chronic stress hurts and even kills. But what can we do about it? Life can be nerve wracking. We live in traumatic times. Money, work problems, family issues, and the economy stress people out more than ever.

You might even take some harder blows, like a divorce, the death of a loved one, a serious accident—automatically, you know you will be unbelievably stressed out. It will be your fate, your destiny to feel overwhelming stress and damage your health if you go through calamities like these. Right?

Well . . . not so fast.

Consider this story told by psychiatrist Peter Johnston of the University of Chicago's student mental health clinic. For thirty years, as a professor and a counselor, Dr. Johnston helped hundreds of angst-prone students—students who found themselves in the midst of what has been called the "the most rigorous, intense learning experience" in America.[22]

I had been counseling a student for several months when I received a phone call. "I won't be at my counseling session today," said the student. "My father just died." Oh no, I thought, how can he possibly cope with this on top of the other stresses he already feels? The student's next comment absolutely astounded me: "Right after the funeral, I have a major examination, so I will contact you after that." "But," I said, "You need time to mourn; you have to give yourself time to emotionally process your father's death. I suggest you put off your exam until you've completed the normal grieving process." "You're right," said the student, "I need time to grieve, but it's not right now. I have an important test to pass or I won't be able to proceed with my career. So, I'm going to concentrate my energies, take the test, and then I will start the grieving process." At that moment, I knew I was dealing with a very mentally sound and strong individual, someone who was in control of his emotions.[23]

Instead of allowing the death of his father—a highly stressful event for most people—to paralyze him, instead of allowing his stress score to go through the roof, he took control of his stress. He decided that life would be in his control instead of life being in control of him. He demonstrated that stress is not inevitable—it's a choice.

And that is the powerful secret of this book: Between any stressor (any kind of *stimulus* that is likely to cause stress) and the actual stress *response* of your body, there is a *gap*, a blessed, sweet, powerful space where you can choose how to respond. In this gap lies your power of free choice and personal control.

Stephen R. Covey describes his discovery of this secret, which took place when he was a college professor:

> One day as I was wandering between stacks of books in the back of the college library, I came across a book that drew my interest. As I opened it, my eyes fell upon a single paragraph that powerfully influenced the rest of my life.
>
> I read the paragraph over and over again. It basically contained the simple idea that *there is a gap or a space between stimulus and response*, and that the key to both our growth and happiness is *how we use that space*.
>
> I can hardly describe the effect that idea had on my mind. The way the idea was phrased—"a gap between stimulus and response"—hit me with fresh, almost unbelievable force. It was like an inward revolution, "an idea whose time had come."
>
> I reflected on it again and again, and it began to have a powerful effect on my paradigm of life. It was as if I had become an observer of my own participation. I began to stand in that gap and to look outside at the stimuli. I reveled in the inward sense of freedom to choose my response.[24]

We have the power to choose our response to any stimulus.

During World War II, the great psychiatrist Viktor Frankl was imprisoned in a concentration camp. It was a desperate, cruel time, but Frankl recalls most of all those prisoners who responded to the brutality with kindness.

> We who lived in concentration camps can remember the men who walked through the huts comforting others, giving away their last piece of bread. They may have been few in number, but they offer sufficient proof that everything can be taken from a man but one thing: the last of the human freedoms—to choose one's attitude in any given set of circumstances, to choose one's own way.[25]

Suppose someone comes up to you and punches you in the face. Your body will start to launch its self-preservation processes, preparing you to punch back. But you can tell your body to cool it. There is a split second (the gap) between when you get punched and when you punch back that can produce amazing consequences for your life. Acting within the gap, you can decide to walk away and bring the altercation to a quick close. Two people can't get in a fight if one of them walks away. Or you can choose to launch your retaliation response. Which approach is likely to leave you with a full set of teeth?

In our community recently, a seventeen-year-old soccer player was given a yellow flag by the referee. The boy looked at the flag and promptly smacked the referee on the side of the head. The referee, a sturdy middle-aged man, was knocked down and seemed to be all right after a few minutes. That night, however, he collapsed; his brain was beginning to swell and hemorrhage. Within a few days he was dead, and the young man may be headed to prison—possibly for many years. The referee's family was left without their dad, and the player's family was devastated. In a fraction of a second, the consequences of our choices in the "gap" can become monumental.

An inmate in a British prison was the target of abuse by a fellow inmate. Finally, after a series of provocations, the abused inmate had had enough. He lay in wait until the abuser was in a place in the prison yard where it was hard for the guards to see. Then he knocked down the man, took out some contraband he had gathered (a lighter and plastic bag of fuel), poured the petrol on the man's face, and flicked on the lighter. As he lowered his hand to ignite the flames, his mind entered the gap.

In a split second, he envisioned another flame, that of the candle on his daughter's birthday cake. He realized that if he proceeded to inflict violence on his fellow inmate, he would never get out of prison to see his daughter's birthday candle. Acting within the gap, he shut the lid on the lighter, got up, and walked away—to the relief and amazement of the fearful man on the ground. Now at his little girl's birthday party, in attendance is her mother—*and her father.* The choice he made in the gap made all the difference.

You can place in the gap a variety of choices that will bring about stress-free responses. Here are some possible examples and the subsequent feeling that happens when you do. We call it upgrading your thoughts. In the gap, upgrade your

- complaining to gratitude and feel joy, serenity, contentment, fun;
- resistance to acceptance/allowance and feel release, relaxation;
- fear to discovery and feel interest, possibility, realization;
- judging to observing and feel calm;

- threats to challenges and feel excitement, eagerness, motivation;
- demands to preferences and feel detachment;
- anger to forgiveness and feel peace;
- guilt to self-acceptance and feel peace, relaxation;
- autobiography to empathy and feel understanding.

WORKOUT: FILLING THE GAP

The purpose of this workout is to help you gain control of the gap between stimulus and response.

Think of an unpleasant situation in which you found yourself getting emotionally upset, angry, frustrated, or stressed.

Consider the following thoughts you could insert into the gap between stimulus and response—the thoughts that would help banish stress.

- Gratitude (I appreciate . . . I am thankful for . . .)
- Allowance/Acceptance (It's okay . . . I embrace this . . . I can live with this . . . I can go with the flow . . .)
- Discovery (I wonder . . . What would happen if . . . What can I learn from this?)
- Observation (I am noticing . . .)
- Challenges (This could be fun . . .)
- Preferences (Even though I'd prefer it this way, I can't control what's happening here . . .)
- Forgiveness (I release my emotional attachment to . . .)
- Self-Acceptance (I'm happy being myself during this . . .)
- Empathy (I'm interested in you . . . I'd like to understand what you're feeling about this . . .)

STRESSBUSTER
Here are some ideas for filling the gap between *stimulus* and *response*:
- Take a deep breath instead of launching into action.
- Ask yourself what you *should* do, not what you want to do.
- Visualize the impact of what you are thinking of doing. What will be the consequence?
- Follow the "golden rule": Treat people with respect and dignity by giving them the benefit of doubt—we all have bad days.
- Forgive.

And it can make all the difference for you.

How so? Are we saying that we can choose to be chronically stressed or not?

That's exactly what we are saying.

It is entirely possible to decide not to be stressed, as Professor Johnston's student demonstrated when he chose to postpone grieving for his father until after his examinations.

We're also saying that many people—maybe most people—are not taking advantage of the gap; they don't control their stress response, even though they have the power to do so. A huge majority of Americans (estimates run between 83 and 91 percent) are stressed out at work.[26] Likewise, in Britain, China, Germany, and Brazil, stress levels are soaring, with the United Kingdom topping the list. At least one-third of British workers are experiencing "unreasonable levels of stress."[27]

Many are actually letting stress kill them. The US Center for Disease Control and Prevention reports that more people in America are now dying from suicide than from car accidents, a 28 percent increase since the turn of the century. Suicides rates nearly doubled in parts of Europe since the financial crisis of 2008.[28] And it is not teenagers who are more likely to take their own lives; it is people between the ages of thirty-five and sixty-four, people in the prime of life who should be enjoying the fruits of adulthood, family, career success, and good health.[29]

WORKOUT: BODY SIGNALS

The purpose of this workout is to make you aware of the signals your body is sending you about stress.

Think about a health concern that you, or someone you know, might be experiencing right now in which stress has likely played a part in its development. This health problem may be a headache, insomnia, or something more serious like depression or ulcers. Based on what you are learning about stress, why might chronic stress be a primary cause of the problem?

Our bodies always give us signals, indicating that we are in balance or out of balance (chronic stress is an imbalanced state). These signals tell us when we've done something that is good for us, like the way we feel after we've worked out, eaten a healthy salad, or helped someone with a problem. We also receive signals from our bodies letting us know when we have chosen unhealthy behaviors, like the hung-over feeling from drinking too much, the stuffed feeling from overeating, or the negative feelings following a stressful argument.

Consider what your body is telling you now about the way you've been treating it. Do you feel perfectly balanced and terrific, or are there conditions you have been struggling with that are telling you that something's not quite right and that stress is the likely culprit?

Next, intentionally participate in a healthy behavior. Examples might include going for a pleasant walk with someone you love; eating a balanced healthy meal, but eating a little less than you normally would; doing something that you thoroughly enjoy with no other motive than to involve yourself in that activity; and helping someone who needs some assistance without letting anyone else know about it.

Focus deliberately on how your body feels during and after doing the healthy activity that you selected. What signals does your body give you, indicating that it was a beneficial activity? Write down your observations somewhere where you can reference them each time you do this workout.

How frequently do you listen to the feedback your body is giving you? When was the last time that you felt terrific? When was the last time your body–mind felt completely centered, balanced, harmonious, and whole? How can you listen more to the wisdom of your body to make choices that help you feel tremendous rather than terrible? We've established that there is an almost immediate physiological stress response when we confront real danger, like a poisonous snake in your path or a car about to collide with yours. But in fact we confront such dangers very rarely. Why then do we respond so automatically—and often disastrously—to far less menacing stressors in our lives? What makes us choose to "stress out" in situations that are clearly not life threatening? Again, from Michael

After explaining to my students the physiology of the stress response, I like to ask them: "As you think back over the last month of your life, how much of your time did you spend in situations where your life was honestly in danger?"

I invite each student to respond. Typically, three or four students will say they went through something serious where their life was in danger, like being in a car accident or running out of air while scuba diving. However, the actual length of these incidents is usually only a few seconds. The amount of time their lives are in real danger is minuscule.

Then I ask them how much of their time they feel symptoms of stress. The response is anywhere from 30 percent to 90 percent.

I always follow this discussion with a final question: *"If you are never really in situations where your life is in danger, why would you ever honestly feel any stress?"*

Keep in mind—absolutely don't forget—the *only* reason for activation of the stress response is to help us escape from a *physically* dangerous situation. So why does our emergency system kick in so strongly and so continuously if we so seldom need it?

The real reason our bodies activate the stress response is that we *interpret* a situation to be potentially painful or threatening, and because of this incorrect interpretation—this false emergency—our bodies gear up for it. Where there is a potential for pain of any kind—a threat thought, emotional, social, or physical—our bodies react in the only way they know to help us survive.

When Sam Bracken was young, everything in life was pain—constant, chronic, emotional pain.

I was born the product of a rape. I grew up hungry and poor, at times living in an orphanage. When my real mother returned for me, things actually got worse. My new stepfather was an alcoholic, a gambler, and a violent abuser. He would beat me for not making his breakfast just right. My stepbrother tormented me, lighting me on fire and encouraging me to do drugs just to see what would happen. At school, I was a failure.

When I was younger and in my teens, I frequently used drugs and alcohol in order to medicate away the unbearable stress of my life. When I was 15, my mother threw me out so she could live with a notorious motorcycle gang on the outskirts of Las Vegas. She was sort of like their den mother.

Today, Sam is a loving father and husband with a distinguished career as a business leader, public speaker, and award-winning author. He became a collegiate football player and is an honors college graduate with an MBA from a top business school. He has held high executive positions with major corporations. He adores his wife and his children, who have distinguished academic and athletic records of their own.

Few of us will ever have to suffer the kind of stresses Sam has faced. How did he unwind his tightly twisted knot of anxiety and discouragement and become the secure and successful individual he is today?

He answers for himself:

I was fortunate. I could have gone through life as a victim, reacting to threats and violence with more threats and violence. I probably would've ended up dead, insane, or in prison. But I learned the key lesson that between the stimulus and response, there is a gap. And in that gap I have perfect freedom to choose my path forward.

Life does not have to consist of fight or flight. We can learn other ways to respond.

Let's find out how.

THE MINDFULNESS RESPONSE

Live fully in the moment.

Every moment of your life has its joys, its beauties to inspire you, its truths to teach. The principle of focus is a basic principle of life. "Mindfulness" means tuning in to those moments. It means paying full attention to what is happening or what you are doing now, focusing the mind on *this moment*. By becoming "mindful," you move into the gap between stimulus and response where you are empowered to choose how you want to experience this moment.

Present-moment focus is challenging for most people. We aren't trained to do this, though it is how we normally functioned when we were very young. The little child embraces each moment, focusing only on what is happening here and now; thus, she doesn't fill her mind up with tomorrow's activities or yesterday's unhappy experience with Mom.

As we matured, we also stopped being mindful and we started being stressed. We figured out how to dwell on next week's deadline or the argument we had last night. Thought in both directions can trigger the stress response because the nervous system doesn't differentiate among past, future, or present events. When we have a threat thought, the nervous system leaps into action to prepare us for the danger. As we've said, that's essential in the moment of danger or great trial, but not for the argument of yesterday or the deadline of next week.

Can we return to that childlike way of thinking where stressful future or past thoughts aren't dominating our consciousness? Yes, and mindfulness is the method.

Let's explore a few truths about the mind that can help you understand "mindfulness."

First, your mind is equipped to focus on only one thing at a time. You might be able to observe many things, but you can think intentionally about only one thing. For example, when you're driving, if you put your focus on your mobile phone, you lose focus on your driving. You can't simultaneously focus on both. (Certainly, you can flip back and forth pretty quickly, but you simply can't do both at the exact same time.)

Second, you're free to think about anything you choose. There are no limits on what you can think about. You aren't stuck with any specific thought about anything.

Third, you can *directly* experience only this moment, right here, right now. You can think about future and past events, but you can't directly experience yesterday's dinner right now. Nor can you experience tomorrow's meeting. We could say that our immediate and direct experience is our only true reality. Everything else is past or future—no longer real or not real yet.

The fourth idea, which we have discussed earlier, is that there is no stress in the present moment, except for very rare occasions (less than .01 percent of the time). We live in societies where we don't directly experience dangerous, life-threatening situations. Here and now is usually a safe place.

If these things are true, and they are, why do we ever become stressed?

We activate the stress response when we send our minds into the future or the past and include threat thoughts into the mix of those future or past thoughts. Worrying, for example, involves thinking of a future event and including a painful scenario in the stream of future thoughts. Regret is essentially doing the same thing but in the opposite direction, into our past.

When we become mindful, we think differently. We bring our mental focus (which, as we stated just a moment ago, can be on only one thing) directly on our current here-and-now experience. We observe the mental data we are receiving. We focus wholly on this moment, right here, right now. It sounds like this:

- What am I *seeing* right now?
- What am I *hearing* right now?
- What am I *sensing* right now?
- What am I *tasting* right now?
- What *thoughts* am I having right now?
- In essence, what am I *currently experiencing*?

And here is why mindfulness is so powerful: The instant we do this, we leave behind threat thoughts of the future or the past, because here and now is safe. As we sense the safety of here and now, the stress response automatically turns off.

Thich Nhat Hanh, a Vietnamese poet and philosopher of mindfulness, challenges our paradigm of stressful activity. He wonders if stress isn't often an illusion. For example, cleaning dishes is generally thought of as an unpleasant task, but he suggests that is simply our paradigm talking. There is another, more peaceful way of looking at it: "I enjoy taking my time with each dish, being fully aware of the dish, the water, and each movement of my hands. I know that if I hurry in order to go and have dessert, the time will be unpleasant, not worth living. That would be a pity, for each minute, each second of life is a miracle. The dishes themselves, and the fact that I am here washing them are miracles! . . . If I am incapable of washing dishes joyfully, if I want to finish them quickly so I can go and have dessert, I will be equally incapable of enjoying my dessert. With the fork in my hands, I will be thinking about what to do next, and the texture and the flavor of the dessert, together with the pleasure of eating it, will be lost. I will always be dragged into the future, never able to live in the present moment."[30]

When we simply observe what is, engaging the mind in what we are seeing or doing at this moment, our minds no longer race with thoughts of the future or the past. *We are just enjoying being in the moment.*

Michael reports on his revelation about mindfulness.

The concept of mindfulness hit me with such power on one occasion that it literally changed my entire outlook on life. I was in the middle of college and had to take a major test that would affect much of my future. I studied like a madman for days and thought I knew all I needed to know.

On the test day, I arrived in the room where about three hundred other people were being tested. It was a tough test, but I was confident. Finally, I submitted my test form and waited around a few minutes to get the results.

Sheer anger, horror, and anguish all hit me at once when I saw that I had gotten a D on the test. I was so upset. How could this professor be so evil? I can't stay in my major with a D! What was I going to do now? I was in deep despair. This was really bad.

As I walked back to my car in this hyperstressed state, I happened to look up. It was late October and the trees were in autumn mode—changing colors brilliantly. In the distance, the sun was setting, its reflection from the lake to the west filling the sky with red and gold hues. Nature offered me a real spectacle that afternoon.

In that moment, I caught myself. I could continue to work myself into a frenzy over a test that was now in the past and worry myself sick over an uncertain future; or I could stop and watch this dazzling display of trees, mountains, lake, and sunset—unparalleled beauty unfolding before me.

I chose to savor the moment.

Walking back to my car, I felt incredibly peaceful. I was different. Really. The joy of the moment displaced my anger and fear. The stress was gone. I figured things would turn out all right—which they did, as they usually do.

How can we learn to focus more fully on the moment?

First, stop. Turn off the mental chatter about what happened and what's going to happen. Hit the pause button. Turn off your mental TV that keeps replaying the same stressful events over and over.

Then look. Attend to what is going on now, at this moment. Don't analyze it, interpret it, judge it, or figure it out. Just stop and look. Tune in to everything that *your senses* are able to capture. To be present in the moment is to be at peace.

You can practice this simple behavior many times a day. For instance, when was the last time you really enjoyed your shower?

Where is your mind when you shower? Are you focusing on how great it feels to get a mini-massage from the spray of water? To feel clean?

Do you have trouble falling asleep? Stressed out over what happened that day or what's going to happen tomorrow? Stop. Focus on the momentary sensations around you and inside of you—warm blankets, cool breeze, darkness, your quiet breathing, your relaxed body. Soon, you'll be out like a light.

Do you really notice what you are eating when you eat? So many people read or watch TV, focusing on something other than the food. Be mentally present at your next meal. Enjoy the sights, smells, and tastes of your food. You'll enjoy it more, you'll digest your food better, and you'll also lower your caloric intake.[31] Michael reports:

> One of my students, Philip, was sitting in my classroom as I walked in. He was eating some yogurt. I asked him how he was doing. "Do you really want to know?" he asked. "Sure," I replied.
>
> He then told me about his troubles. He was struggling with his relationship with his wife. His business partner was suing him. He had two huge tests coming up and a couple of big papers due next week. He said he was really stressed out and weighed down. "What do you think I should do, Doc?" he asked.
>
> After a moment of thought, I responded: "Philip, I think you should enjoy your yogurt."

Now, whether or not Philip enjoyed his yogurt wouldn't change the reality he lived with, the things that had happened or would happen in the future. What it would do was change his paradigm of that moment. It would de-stress him and perhaps even give him more perspective on what was happening, instead of the impulse to run or fight. That's what mindfulness can do.

Alan Watts, the English philosopher, captured the essence of mindfulness with this thought:

> No one imagines that a symphony is supposed to improve as it goes along, or that the whole object of playing is to reach the finale. The point of music is discovered in every moment of playing and listening to it. It is the same, I feel, with the greater part of our lives, and if we are unduly absorbed in improving them we may forget altogether to live them.[32]

Most of you reading this book live a busy life. We have a lot of things on our plates. And for some of us, we can't really afford to take too many things off the plate—we are involved in a lot of very important things. Consider the single mother with children who need her. She works professionally, tries to maintain a comfortable home, and wants to get in some exercise and to spend some time with a friend who needs her listening ear. It's easy for her to get stressed thinking about all the things she has to do and to worry about getting everything done. How can she possibly handle it all without stressing out?

Of course, careful planning and prioritizing make a big difference, as we'll see later. Planning is bringing future events into the present so that we can apply appropriate control. If we don't plan, the important things simply won't happen.

But once the planning is in place, once the future event is in our control to the extent that we can control it, it's time to stop thinking about it and return to the present, enjoying what is happening here and now.

When we function mindfully, we put all of our attention *only* on what is happening each moment, without filling up those moments with thoughts of future and past. When the single mother is at a child's soccer match, she is fully present for it. When she is taking a child to a music lesson, she fully enjoys her time with the child. When she is at work, she focuses on her work to the exclusion of everything else. When she is spending quality time with her friend, all of her attention is on helping her friend.

Psychologist Jon Kabat-Zinn reminds us that "mindfulness involves intentionally doing only one thing at a time and making sure I am here for it."[33]

Mindfulness implies that we cease consuming the present by beating ourselves up over the past and the future. Remember, we can focus only on one thing at a time. The present moment, here and now, is not stressful. The past and the future can be. But you have a choice about which one you want to think about.

WORKOUT: MINDFUL EATING

The purpose of this workout is to help you focus on eating more mindfully, which is a proven stress reducer.

When we eat, typically we shove food into our mouths thoughtlessly, take a few brief chews of that food, and send the only partly chewed food down to the stomach to work overtime on those portions that have hardly been broken down. It's no wonder we get tired after a meal.

The following activity breaks us out of that mode of eating.

When you have some time, go *by yourself* to a place that serves food that you love. It doesn't matter what kind of food or what kind of restaurant you choose. It only matters that you are by yourself and that the food appeals to you.

Experience this food mindfully. Focus on the experience of eating your food to the exclusion of everything else. Focus on the taste of each bite as it touches parts of your tongue to explode with flavor.

Focus on the joy and wonder of allowing this food to literally become a part of you. Tune in to all of the smells and varieties of tastes that you encounter.

WORKOUT: FULL MINDFULNESS

The purpose of this workout is to allow you to experience full mindfulness, using your ability to observe with all of your senses.

The next time that you notice stress taking hold of your thoughts, emotions, and even your physiology, here's something you can do wherever you are. Don't try to do any more than this. It's so simple you might not think it works. It does, every time.

1. Release your mind from the thoughts you're having that are bringing on the stress. As much as possible, consciously push the "Stop" button to the endlessly repeating unpleasant thoughts. Consciously decide that you don't have to think those thoughts anymore. This may not always seem so easy. Fortunately, step 2 is very easy.

2. Put all of your awareness into your senses, and observe what shows up as you tune in to your immediate

environment. With all of your awareness, tune in to the following:

a. What you see right here, right now. Really observe things in your immediate environment. Don't look *for* anything; just look, notice, observe. Become interested in the varieties of things that you notice as you look around. Get into the details of the varieties. For example, if you're observing a tree, notice the different colors of the leaves, the variety of colors of the tree bark, how the tree connects with the ground, and how the color of the ground is a different color. Observe the tree as it compares with other trees in your immediate vicinity. Observe the varieties of leaves on the trees. Notice how wide, tall, short, stumpy, or spread out the tree is. Be interested in how short you are in relation to the tree. Notice the contrast of the green tree to the blue sky.

b. What you hear right here, right now. What sounds are going on? Focus entirely on all the environmental sounds that present themselves to you. Are there car sounds, people talking? Tune in to the sound of the breeze or the birds chirping. Be as detailed observing the sounds as you are with the sights.

c. What you smell right here, right now. Focus your awareness on all the smells of your immediate environment. Perhaps there aren't any obvious ones, but as you tune in to that sense, you notice subtle smells drifting through your space.

d. What you touch right here, right now. Use your hands and the rest of your skin to tune in to everything you can feel. How do your shoes feel against the bottom and top of your feet? Notice your other clothes as they sit on your body. Experiment with your hands and fingers touching this or that thing, and notice the differences and similarities. You could also passively observe the various parts of your body and just notice any subtle or obvious sensations that are happening in any part.

    e. What you taste right here, right now. Notice your tongue resting in your mouth. Can you still taste any remnant of food from your last meal or snack? Try eating something and thoroughly experience the taste. Stay focused on the flavor, the texture, the firmness or softness of the food. Notice the differences in the flavors as you introduce one food and then another. Observe what's in your mouth from a very interested perspective.

3. Let go of your need to judge anything that you observe. Observe everything that presents itself to your senses the same way you would look at a rainbow, a starry night, or a sunset without judging, analyzing, or comparing. If you notice any stressful thoughts creeping back in, return to a full focus on your senses.

Congratulations! You have just experienced the master skill of mindfulness!

When you are finished, record your experience by responding to the following:

- What setting did you select for your mindfulness activity? Why?

- What were some of the main things that you observed, especially those things you wouldn't normally notice?
- What did you notice about your thoughts?
- What did you notice about your feelings?
- What insights did you gain about yourself and about mindfulness as you were practicing being mindful?
- What did you notice about your stress levels as you immersed yourself fully in your experience?

Remember, becoming mindful is like any mental muscle. It gets stronger with use. This activity will help you work this mental muscle very powerfully.

THE POWER OF PARADIGMS

Everyone thinks of changing the world,
but no one thinks of changing himself.

—Leo Tolstoy

In the gap between stimulus and response is your power to choose your own response.

If you choose to respond mindfully, you focus on the present moment rather than dwelling on the past or the future. In that mindful space, in that moment, you are exercising your greatest human gift—*your power to think about what you are thinking.*

For example, most people say rush hour in the city can be very stressful—especially if you're late for something important to you. But is it possible to be in a car or bus or train crawling along at low speed in a crowded city and *not* feel anxious about it?

Of course it's possible. It always depends on how you think about it. *No event in life, short of a life- or limb-threatening situation, is inherently stressful.* It always depends on how you *interpret* the event, whether it stresses you or not. Between the external stimulus and your response to it is the gap in which you can choose to dismiss stress from your life.

You do it by challenging your *paradigm* about the stimulus.

Let us explain. Your paradigm is the lens through which you see the world outside—not in terms of your visual sense of sight, but in term of perceiving, understanding, and interpreting. If your "lens"—your paradigm—is distorted, you will see things in a distorted way. It's like wearing the wrong pair of glasses.

For example, an acquaintance of ours was mortally afraid of dogs. He liked to walk for relaxation, but if he saw or even heard a dog, he would change his route immediately, looking around in panic for a different way to go. One time a dog ran toward him and he nearly lost his mind, screaming for the owner to leash that animal! His paradigm of dogs was that they were vicious beasts who would tear his throat out if they got close enough.

But for a long time his little daughter coaxed and cried for a dog as a pet. Because he loved his daughter, he figured he could tolerate a small, unthreatening dog. A little English Spaniel took up residence. Our friend was surprised when the dog began to pay more attention to him than to his daughter: The dog would nuzzle and lick him and demand to be petted by him. At first he was apprehensive, but by all appearances the dog loved him. Soon his experience of the dog's affection, the warm and relaxed feeling of cuddling the dog, the delight he felt when the dog went crazy with joy at the sight of him—all this changed his whole attitude toward dogs. He began to welcome the sight of a dog on his walk through the city. He would walk up to it and talk to it, pet it, and admire it. He found that most pet dogs were delightfully friendly to him, and he quickly lost his former fears.

What happened to our friend? Why did something that had stressed him so deeply no longer stress him at all?

His paradigm about dogs changed radically.

How did it happen?

First, note that dogs themselves were *not* the problem. Of course, some dogs are vicious, but the vast majority of domesticated pets being walked on the streets of a modern city are harmless. Real dogs didn't cause him stress—his *paradigm* of dogs caused him stress.

Second, the original paradigm was what psychologists call a "conditioned response." Maybe dogs had frightened our friend as a child; maybe he was just scared of their loud bark and sharp teeth—whatever the original reason, he had developed a habit of responding to the stimulus in a way that didn't correspond to reality. Dogs "pushed his buttons," as we say.

Everyone has different "stress buttons": a boss, a neighbor's loud music, heavy traffic, crowds, a certain customer's demands. An acquaintance of ours is deeply stressed by mountains—she can't sleep, her stomach hurts, and she gets visibly restless when in the vicinity of a mountain. She's afraid it will fall on her. Yet most people love mountain scenery.

Now, many people experience phobias and depression of various kinds that are similar to stress. Research suggests that clinical mental problems rarely have simple causes. Genetics, medications, addictions, real trauma, complex brain chemistry—these forces interact in ways that are unique to each individual. Sam remembers this:

When he was thirteen, my son ran around a corner in our house and slipped on a sock. He crashed the back of his head on the hard laminate floor. The hospital treated him and said he'd be okay. But he wasn't.

Powerfully built, highly competitive, incredibly musical, my son became the kid everybody liked in high school. He played football and was very successful at it, but unfortunately he took a few more hits to the head.

In later years, he began waking up in a panicky state. Then he couldn't sleep, couldn't study, and couldn't concentrate. Psychiatrists put him on depression medication, but he seemed to get worse. A sense of despair and anxiety came over him to the point where he was incapable of doing anything at all.

I knew about the 'fight-or-flight' response, but I had never seen someone simply freeze with despair.

I tried to get him to snap out of it by being strict with him and sometimes even harsh. That didn't work. I tried to teach him about mantra meditation, guided imagery, soothing music—he couldn't find comfort in any of it. "Dad, I wake up in a panic and it never goes away." If he couldn't find the exact pair of workout shorts he wanted to wear, he would scream profanities and punch the wall with his fists.

Then I started reading about stress and anxiety and learned a little about brain injuries. We took him to a specialized clinic where they scanned his brain electronically.

The bad news was that he did indeed have a traumatic brain injury. Scans revealed lesions from the incident when he was thirteen. Specialists said he had the brain of a retired professional football player. It was not necessarily an emotional disorder—it was brain damage.

The good news was that we could help him heal.

The specialists helped enormously. An anti-seizure medication calmed his injured brain. Hyperbaric chamber treatments sped up nerve healing. Included in the prescription were restful sleep, a lot of water, resistance training with weights, aerobic exercise, and racket sports to improve eye-hand coordination.

After several weeks we began to get our son back.

Of course, our family members were stressed out of their minds too. Everyone was pressing the stress button, and the strain was palpable in the house. How were we supposed to overcome *our* anxieties?

So the family is also going through cognitive behavior therapy—essentially the stressbusting paradigms and skills we teach in this book. We learned that our son's arguments, the attacks, the wild gestures were actually his outlets for anxiety—the "fight" response. So we were counseled to surround him with love and acceptance, to be firm, kind, and "nudging" him to do better. When he gets abusive, we speak kindly to him. We can't speak in anger because it makes things worse.

We started rallying around him. We changed our diet to include more green vegetables and lean meats, played light classical music at home, went for massages, put in aromatherapy diffusers through the house to provide a calming atmosphere.

These paradigm shifts are helping our family. But my son needed more than a paradigm shift—he needed attention to his brain injury.

Even professionals are often unsure where the line is between actual brain illness and the anxieties we experience due to faulty paradigms. If you suffer from anxiety that significantly affects your relationships and your performance at work, you need to seek a physician's help.

In everyday life, however, our paradigms play a huge role in whether we stress out or not.

One person can drive happily at a snail's pace through city traffic, whereas another will stress out to the boiling point. One person can be perfectly content with a business decision, whereas another will chafe and grumble and spit blame in all directions.

What pushes your buttons? What stimuli do you automatically respond to by getting stressed out? Now, you can change your paradigm about any stimulus. Our dog-fearing friend changed his paradigm as a result of a new kind of conditioning—he got to know and love a real dog. This paradigm shift sort of happened by itself, but you can *make* it happen for yourself. You do it by identifying and challenging the paradigms that are causing you stress.

STRESSBUSTER

The next time you are feeling really stressed out, ask yourself these mindful questions:

- "Is my life in danger?"
- "What is the real threat here?"
- "What is happening now?"

For example, you're hung up in traffic and late for a meeting. You are going to be physically safe when you arrive at the meeting, and you are certainly safe sitting in your comfortable car in the traffic jam. The perceived threat is that you are going to be late and bad things might happen when you arrive. Certainly, being late to the meeting will have its ramifications, but there's no real physical danger when you get there or while you're sitting in traffic.

If your life is not in danger and you can handle being late, turn up the music and relax using the techniques you're going to learn in this book.

We call it "unwinding." If you're stressed out, your paradigms have you all wound up inside, and you need to unwind them, examine them, and replace them with new paradigms that leave you unstressed. Just as our friend's paradigm about dogs unraveled, so can your stress-inducing paradigms.

Michael has this story:

We arrived on time for an important soccer match one Saturday afternoon. Our daughter was playing, and we were ready to go. Uncharacteristically, one of the referees was late, and the match couldn't proceed without him.

As the minutes ticked by, the crowd became more and more stressed. One voice complained how disrespectful the official was; another said he had better things to do than to wait around for this guy to show up. People planned nasty things to say to him if he ever did arrive. The tension grew by the minute.

Then a mobile phone rang. The official's son had been seriously injured in an auto accident, and he would be late. He apologized for the delay.

There was a collective and instantaneous change in the crowd. Feelings of anger and frustration turned immediately into expressions of love and concern for this man and his son. The paradigm shifted 180 degrees.

The surly crowd had been stressed out by a distorted paradigm. They misunderstood the reality of the situation and really made no attempt to challenge that paradigm until it was changed for them by one phone call.

The rest of this book is about challenging or "unwinding" the paradigms that are causing you stress—taking them out for an airing, examining them closely, and replacing them with paradigms that work better for you.

WORKOUT: ARE YOU REALLY IN DANGER?

The purpose of this workout is to help you realize how infrequently you really experience actual threats to your life.

You will be doing some math so you may need a calculator.

Start by thinking about the previous month of your life—every waking moment. Next, think back to any events that you experienced when your life was honestly in danger, or someone you were with was in danger. Situations like having an argument with a family member or being late to work or anything of this nature are *not* life threatening (though you may have felt stress). You are looking only for situations that are the equivalent of a big angry bear running toward you. Then enter the number of seconds or minutes you spent in life-threatening situations in the calculator and add them up.

For example, maybe you almost got hit by a car. The actual time that this took was probably two or three seconds in total. Nothing else counts that occurred surrounding the incident, such as the thoughts you had as you continued walking safely on your way. Consider only the timing of the incident itself.

Next, divide the accumulated number of seconds or minutes that were truly life threatening into the total amount of time you lived last month. Divide the seconds by 2,592,000 or the minutes by 43,200 minutes. What's the resulting percentage of time in life-threatening situations?

Your results will probably add up to far less than 1 percent. In reality, very little of our lives are spent in situations that require the stress response. We are very rarely in life-threatening situations. Now ask yourself these two very important questions:

- Earlier, you completed several self-assessments. One of them was the stress-o-meter in which you gave yourself a general stress score of some number between 1 and 10 (10 being extremely high stress). Was the score that you gave yourself higher than a 2 or a 3?
- If you are so infrequently in situations that are life threatening and the stress response has only one function, which is to help you survive life-threatening situations, *why would you ever feel stress?*

Take a few minutes to think through and perhaps write down your thoughts and feelings as you consider these two questions.

SHIFTING THE STRESS PARADIGMS

There are basic principles of effective living, and people can only experience true success and enduring happiness as they learn and integrate these principles into their basic character.
—*Stephen R. Covey*

There are seven paradigms you need to change if you want to reduce or eliminate stress in your life. They were identified years ago by Dr. Stephen R. Covey.

When Dr. Covey published his famous book *The 7 Habits of Highly Effective People*, he had no idea that the book would sell twenty-five million printed copies and fifteen million audio copies, as well as be considered by many as the most influential book written in the last century. In this book, he laid out some of the basic principles of effective living, such as integrity, resourcefulness, foresight, compassion, and empathy for others.

What does that book have to do with stress?

Simply, people who live by the principles of effectiveness suffer from far less negative stress in their lives because they don't do the things that produce negative stress. Their paradigms don't induce stress; they eliminate stress. These people "have a set of positive conditioned responses to stimuli." More to the point, these people live more purposeful lives, disentangled from indecision and worry.

The natural consequence of living according to these principles is tranquility. However, for many of us, we first have to move ourselves out of the chronically stressed mode and back into balance. Once there, we can move toward tranquility, a state of lasting inner peace and harmony.

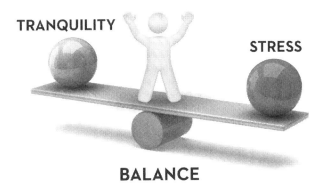

Just about all of the stress people experience comes from inside themselves, rather than outside. They might have a victim mentality. They fail at foresight—no plans, no budgets, no grasp of how to prepare for the future. They lack the ability to prioritize things in their lives, and as a result they get overloaded and overwhelmed. They might have trouble relating to other people because they have a paradigm of defensiveness or egotism. They don't know how to say no. Often they are not even aware of these harmful paradigms.

There are seven very common, but also very stress-inducing, paradigms that you must change if you're going to move from stress to tranquility in your life,

Paradigm 1: From Reactive to Proactive. Most people have the paradigm of reactivity. They react to stress-inducing stimuli as if they had no choice but to be stressed out. With the paradigm of proactivity, you are mindful. You recognize that you can always choose your response "in the gap." Also, you can be proactive about stress by planning for it and preventing it. In other words, you take control of your own life instead of letting outside forces control you.

Paradigm 2: From Unmotivated to Inspired. Most stressed-out people have no vision or purpose, no sense of the end to which they are working (or if they once had it they've lost sight of it in the day-to-day struggle). They mindlessly wait for some outside force to "motivate" them. With the paradigm of inspiration, you create your own clear "end in mind" and you do not let yourself lose sight of it. Because you are deeply committed to your vision, you simply don't experience the hopelessness so many stressed-out people experience.

Paradigm 3: From Pressures to Priorities. Stressed-out people almost always complain about being overwhelmed with things to do. They have the paradigm of pressure—they are under pressure, they live with pressure, they are flattened by pressure. With a paradigm of priorities, you set a few important priorities and place everything else on the back burner. You no longer have "too much to do." *You* decide where to invest your time and energy—nobody else.

Paradigm 4: From Hassles to Harmony. Stressed-out people talk about being "hassled" by others. The British call it *aggro* (for aggravation) and the French call it *embêtement*, and it's something other people do to you. If you have the paradigm of harmony, you're not hassled because you're always looking for mutual benefit with others—for the harmony that comes when everyone "wins," including you.

Paradigm 5: From Anxiety to Empathy. Much of the stress we experience comes from misunderstanding, a word we often use for "a big fight" once it's over. Social stress is the most common kind of stress. Socially stressed people might withdraw, and their "cocooning" behavior makes them depressed and more likely to develop heart disease, stroke, and diabetes. If you have the paradigm of empathy, you truly understand others. You understand not only what they think but also what they feel, and they know you do. This skill has the miraculous effect of draining the tension out of a strained relationship.

Paradigm 6: From Defensive to Diverse. We live in angry times. There's a lot of shouting in the media, a lot of distrustful tribalism, and not much tolerance of differences. People try to cope with the stressful times by becoming defensive, which ironically just makes them more stressed. But if you have the paradigm of diversity, you actually welcome different people, opinions, and contributions. When people can capitalize on their differences instead of defending themselves from differences, we get creative solutions to stressful problems.

Paradigm 7: From Tense to Tranquil. A carpenter who never stops sawing will soon have a dull saw. Likewise, people whose "stress switch" is always on need skills that can turn the switch off. We will give you a whole repertory of these skills that will help you move from tension to tranquility.

In this book, we're going to dive deep into each of these paradigm shifts, which will help you prevent most of the daily stresses people typically experience, by getting at the roots of the things that cause stress. Most books on stress management are about coping with stress when it attacks. This book is to a great extent about preventing stress in the first place.

Of course, you can't prevent all the negative stress in your life. The world is too unpredictable for that. So you will also find in this book many wonderful techniques for calming your symptoms when stress occurs despite your best efforts to prevent it. Some of these stress-reducing activities also show up throughout this book in the form of Stressbusters and Workouts.

Let's find out just how the seven paradigms are affecting you. This short Stress Quiz will help you gauge how stressed you really are. Simply consider how often you feel these things.

WORKOUT: THE 7 PARADIGMS

In the last month, how often have you felt that things in your life were getting out of control?

Answer with never, almost never, fairly often, or very often. You will be referring back to this Workout often.

- Things in your life were getting out of control?
- Unmotivated to "get up and go"?
- Difficulty coping with all the things you have to do?
- You are "losing ground" in your life?
- Other people are making you anxious?

- Defensive or angry?
- Stressed out because of something that happened unexpectedly?

If you find that you have experienced these feelings fairly or very often, you are experiencing seriously and possibly dangerous levels of stress.

We promise that if you will carefully follow the simple recommendations in this book, a couple of wonderful things will happen. First, you will notice a decrease in your symptoms of stress right away. You'll feel immediate relief from your stress as you start putting into play the activities and behaviors that we outline for you.

Second, and more importantly, as you incorporate into your life the principles, paradigms, and practices in this book, you will develop a way of being that is peaceful, happy, and filled with joy. Being stress free will be the way that you *are*, rather than feeling so stressed all the time. It will no longer be a struggle.

In our experience, it will take about ten weeks for this to happen. Why ten? According to researchers at the University of London's Epidemiology and Public Health program, it takes an average of sixty-six days to form a new habit.[34] Unless you form new habits—new "conditioned responses"—you will likely stay stressed. But if you practice what is taught here, you should be relatively stress free in less than three months.

PART 2

HOW TO LIVE A
STRESS-FREE LIFE

FROM REACTIVE
TO PROACTIVE

No one is free who has not obtained the empire of himself.
—Pythagoras

About two weeks ago I had reached the lowest point I have ever reached in my entire life and I was actually contemplating suicide. Correction, I wasn't contemplating suicide, I was going to commit suicide. I started to think about how the world had done this to me, why I was so unlucky. And then I saw your stress management textbook sitting on the table, and I started to read about how stress is not real, about how it is just a perception that we choose to acknowledge. I kept reading for over an hour. I was overwhelmed with this feeling of control, that I could control my emotions, and my emotions didn't have to control me. I felt that I could take control of my life. I've started eating healthier and exercising, and I've started seeing a therapist to help work through things. I feel like I am learning how to live in the moment and not in the past and not to worry about the future.

This candid memo to Dr. Olpin captures the most important thing we can teach you about stress management: Stress is not real. You might feel like arguing against that, especially when you find yourself unable to sleep at night, incapable of remembering even simple tasks, and sweating through scary, irregular heartbeats. Such symptoms may make stress seem very real to you. But in a sense, you have *chosen* to be stressed.

> **STRESSBUSTER**
> Understand that *feelings* are not always *facts*. At times our feelings can distort our paradigm or point of view of reality.
> The next time you feel stressed out about something, ask yourself, "Is this really a life-threatening issue? Is the thing I'm stressed out about really worth the emotional energy I'm giving to it? Will all my frazzled feelings change the situation in any way?"

Look closely at the message. "I was going to commit suicide. I started to think about how the world had done this to me, why I was so unlucky." The world had it in for him. He had no "luck." The universe was against him. It was *making* him commit suicide.

Of course, these observations are irrational. The individual had developed a paradigm of himself as a victim, and his perception of the events of his life reinforced that paradigm. It is the same paradigm behind so many of the things we say when we're stressed out:

"He makes me so mad."
"I can never catch a break."
"I'm such a loser."
"That's just the way I am."
"There's nothing I can do about it."
"My life sucks."

We call this way of thinking the reactive paradigm because it's typical of people who react to the world around them as if they had no responsibility themselves. Forces external to themselves—luck, fate, destiny, the boss, the wife, the boyfriend, the government, the "system"—are to blame for their stress. They do not act; they react. They do not control their own lives; they are controlled.

According to researchers, stress reactivity contributes to obesity, heart disease, depression, and social withdrawal. Reactive people have a low stress threshold—they are often stressed out by small problems, and big problems simply defeat them.[35]

The reactive paradigm is distorted. Human beings are not inert objects to be acted upon. Unlike a rock that has no choice but to roll if it is kicked down a hill, we are free to choose our response to any stimulus. No one can "make" us mad or sad or glad. Unless they're using physical duress, no one can make us do anything against our will. In the absence of some debilitating trauma or mental condition that impairs our free will, we choose to be mad or sad or glad. The reactive paradigm is the "mindless" paradigm.

The opposite paradigm is the paradigm of proactivity. It is the "mindful" paradigm. A proactive person acts instead of reacting. She recognizes that she has the freedom to choose. She uses her own initiative to make things happen instead of waiting for things to happen by themselves. She is self-reliant.

Her real power, however, is in her mindfulness—in her ability to stop and challenge her own paradigms. The proactive person questions her own assumptions as well as those of others. You can hear proactivity in her voice:

"We don't have to take no for an answer."
"There are always options. What are our options?"
"So what if we don't have enough resources. What resources *do* we have?"
"Can I think about this in a different way?"
"We just haven't talked to the right people yet."

In the reactive paradigm, your life feels dictated by external forces, and you have little or no control over them. Those forces "stress you out." But in the proactive paradigm, your life is dictated by you. You, and no one else, control your life. You choose how you will respond to stressful circumstances. You choose to feel some other way than stressed.

According to the best science, "people who believe that events are contingent on unknown or uncontrollable causes (like powerful others, chance, luck, or fate) seem to be debilitated by obstacles or failures. They are more upset and show greater involuntary stress reactions."[36] In other words, people with the reactive paradigm are far more stressed out than they need to be. The root of their stress is their beliefs.

> **STRESSBUSTER**
> Bad things happen to good people every day. Life is a gamble. Sometimes bad things happen to us because we make bad decisions; sometimes bad things happen to us because of random chance; sometimes we're in a bad place at the wrong time.
> When something bad happens to you, pay attention to your inner dialogue. Change it to something like this: "What is happening to me right now does not seem good, but I can choose to respond to it in a better way." The most important conversations you will ever have are the ones you have with yourself.

We have an acquaintance who recently graduated from law school, took the bar exam, and passed it with no trouble. At the same time, his wife was offered a job in another state, so they moved. He was able to get a good position at a law firm; but to represent clients in court, he had to take the bar exam again in his new location. He studied morning and night to get up to speed on laws that were new to him, but unfortunately he failed the exam by a few points—and he was totally stressed out! Hearing him, you would have thought the world was coming to an end.

But his world wasn't coming to an end. His wife had a good job; he had a good job; his new firm was willing to continue his employment until he could take the exam again in a few months; and the odds were that after practicing law in his new state for a few more months, he would be able to pass the exam easily next time. So there was no immediate threat to his livelihood.

Still the lawyer was stressed out. Remember, stress is the body's natural way of protecting itself from *immediate physical danger*. He was not in immediate danger, so his stress response was inappropriate and unreasonable. In fact, it was more than that; it was unhealthy. Eventually, his choice to stress out continually over this failure damaged his immune system and made him seriously depressed and ill.

The lawyer's reactive paradigm was out of kilter with reality. Proactive people, by contrast, have the power to challenge their own paradigms to see if they line up with reality. Instead of challenging his own paradigm, the lawyer chose to ignore the reality of his situation and to stay stressed.

WORKOUT: THE WORLD IS NOT A STRESSFUL PLACE

The purpose of this workout is to help you realize that the real cause of your stress is not what you think it is.

Imagine for a moment that your boss becomes ill, and you are called on to give the important presentation the boss was going to give to some very significant people. Now answer these questions:

- How would you feel if you were getting ready to give this presentation in front of all these very important people? Would you feel nervous, anxious, scared, panicked?
- If you were at home, talking to your family; or in a café, talking to your best friend and saying the same things, would you feel the same kind of stress?
- So, if you are doing virtually the same thing in both places—just talking—why would talking to an audience feel so uncomfortable, whereas talking to friends wouldn't?
- Why would you feel stressed in one place and not the other?
- Is there ever any threat of physical pain or death while you are standing in front of this group of people giving a presentation? (The correct answer is no.)
- If you are never in any danger, what was it about your experience that makes you feel stressed in front of an audience?

We learn from this example that it is rarely the situation or the event that causes us to feel stress, but instead the way we interpret what is happening. The world is not a stressful place; there are only stressful *interpretations* of a world that is, by and large, unthreatening. Of course there are exceptions, but as we discovered earlier, they happen only rarely.

Of course, reality can seem depressing, as in this account of a New Yorker on his way to work at the City University of New York (CUNY):

He'd waited for half an hour on a packed subway platform, and then given up and taken a bus. There was an incident on the bus—accusations of pickpocketing, denials, tumult, delay. He got off and walked the remaining seventeen blocks. A man was running in and out of traffic, laughing and waving his arms about wildly. He almost got hit. It was freezing cold. The night before he had gone to a movie alone. A man a few rows ahead kept turning around and staring at him. The movie was about how miserable life can be. There was a disturbed-looking youth at a Burger King where he went next. On the wall of his apartment building there was a sign warning against crime. During the night he heard a terrible car crash. Next day the street was full of garbage. The woman running the newsstand screamed at him. Finally after an hour and a half of travel he reached the CUNY lobby where he saw a sign advertising a lecture, "Stressors in the Workplace."[37]

Still, this New Yorker had the choice to allow these events to stress him out or not.

People with the proactive paradigm are just less prone to stress. Instead of trying to cope with continual stress, they choose to avoid stress in the first place. Psychologists call this "proactive coping." "The primary advantages of proactive coping likely involve the more modest resource costs of addressing problems earlier in their course and the corresponding reduction in exposure to stress . . . proactive coping may serve to keep chronic stress under control by building

Dr. Michael Olpin and Sam Bracken

resources in advance, by preserving resources through effective early management of potential problems, and by reducing an individual's total stress exposure."[38] In other words, it's easier to unwind if you already have the resources to deal with it.

Now, don't get us wrong. Proactive people don't just *avoid* stressful situations—like everyone else, they never know what will happen to them. But they do things to make stress less likely. Proactive people know that even though they can't control the external world, the external world doesn't control *them*. They are secure in the knowledge that there are certain principles in life that are timeless and unchanging—and they seek to live by those principles.

Living a principle-centered life is the best stress-prevention tool we know.

For example, you can help avoid the stress of financial insecurity by living within your means and saving for the future. You can also get a solid education and qualify for a well-paying job. The basic principles of economics can't be violated without stressful consequences.

You can help prevent "overwhelm" by saying no to things that are less important. The basic principles of time management can't be violated without stressful consequence.

You can help avoid the stress of poor health by exercising, eating right, getting regular checkups, and avoiding addictions that are known to degrade your health. The basic principles of health can't be violated without stressful consequences.

You can help avoid the stress of strained relationships by being kind, respectful, forgiving, and generous. The basic principles of human relations can't be violated without stressful consequences.

Now, you can't avoid any of these sources of stress without being proactive. That too is an inescapable and obvious principle.

Dr. Covey said, "The principles that govern human effectiveness—natural laws in the human dimension—are just as real, just as unchanging and unarguably 'there' as laws such as gravity are in the physical dimension."[39]

We believe there is far more chronic stress in most people's lives from abandoning or fudging on true principles than from moments of physical danger. The principles we're talking about include preparation, economy, initiative, and resourcefulness. But we're also talking about ethical principles: honesty, integrity, loyalty, kindness, forgiveness, patience, and humility. People who align their paradigms with ethical principles are far less likely to experience stress.

STRESSBUSTER

When you're stressed out, pause to take a personal inventory:

What natural laws or principles are you not paying attention to, or even violating?

- Mental?
- Physical?
- Social/emotional?
- Spiritual?

We like this quotation from that great book *Ethics for Dummies*:

Lives that are lived ethically tend to be calmer, more focused, and more productive than those that are lived unethically. Most people can't turn off their sympathy for other human beings. Hurting people leaves scars on both the giver and the receiver. As a result, unethical people have stormier internal lives because they have to work to suppress their consciences and sympathies to deal with the ways they treat others. When they fail to properly suppress their sympathies, the guilt and shame that comes with harming or disrespecting one's fellow human beings takes deep root within them.[40]

Honest people who act with integrity are less likely to experience emotional turmoil over their own behavior. Over time, they live with less guilt, less internal contradiction. Forgiving people are less likely to waste their energies on grudges and politics. Patient people are less likely to stress out over adversity, accidents, illness, and so on.

As we've seen, stress ends when the body returns to physical homeostasis. There's also such a thing as *moral homeostasis*—internal stability around principles like integrity, self-worth, and empathy. Internal stability means aligning our paradigms with principles.

So how do we get to moral homeostasis?

Aristotle said, "Moral virtue comes about as a result of habit . . . None of the moral virtues is engendered in us by nature . . . their full development in us is due to habit." We develop the proactive paradigm through conscious decisions made in the space between stimulus and response.

For example, after many years of marriage and several children, the husband of a friend of ours unexpectedly left her and the children. She suddenly became a single mother who had to cope with the emotional pain both she and the children were experiencing, while simultaneously handling the household tasks and her full-time job. Her friends were blunt about the divorce settlement; they urged retaliation. "Take him to the cleaners," they said. "Show him what it's like to be dumped on."

You might think that she was tempted to do just that. From all accounts, she had been a good wife and did not deserve what her husband had done to her. She might have entered into a period of high stress and anxiety as she struggled with how to handle the details of the divorce—should she get revenge or not? But she did not struggle. Many years before, she had made a decision to live by the principle that everyone deserves respect. She believed that even in difficult circumstances, even when people do unkind and hurtful things, they should be treated with civility and kindness. That is how she treated her former husband; consequently, she and her children made it through those difficult times with very few scars and comparatively little stress.

What you can't control

THINGS ABOVE THE CLOUDS

THINGS BELOW THE CLOUDS

What you can control

Think of things you cannot control as "above the clouds." You can't really do much about them, if anything—natural disasters, wars, the economy, accidents. Now think of things you *can* control as "below the clouds." You can do something to prepare for disasters, wars, or economic problems. You can do things to minimize the chance of accidents. So live "below the clouds" and stop stressing out about things "above the clouds."

In your life, there are many things you can't control. Studies show conclusively that lack of control is related to stress. It is an inverse relationship: The more you are in control of your life, the less stress you feel; and the less you are in control, the more stress you feel. The abandoned wife was not in control of what happened to her. She could have driven her stress levels—and those of everyone around her—through the roof. But her response to the abandonment was *entirely* in her control. She chose to act on a basic principle of human relations: civility and respect. No one could *make* her act otherwise, and the result was far less stressful than it could have been.

The same is true of you. Though you can't always control the stimulus, you can control your response to it. With the proactive paradigm, you can control your emotions; they don't have to control you. You can decide to act on principles—the timeless, unchangeable truths of life.

If you want to unwind, decide *now* to become proactive about your life. Use this Proactivity Workout to make it happen.

WORKOUT: PROACTIVITY

The purpose of this workout is to help you to become more proactive rather than being reactive and stressed out.

Earlier we asked, "How often in the last month have you felt that things in your life were getting out of control?"

If you answered "fairly often" or "very often," you are experiencing high amounts of stress in this area. The goal is to be able to say "almost never" or even "never."

Work through this exercise and refer to your answers every day for at least two months. Ask yourself each day how you are doing with the steps you commit to take.

If you're stressed about finances, what principles should you work on?

- Spending less than I earn
- Saving money for emergencies

What steps could you take to make these principles part of your life?

- Make a budget
- Set up a savings account

Ask yourself the same questions about:

- Work
- Health
- Weight
- Relationships
- Family
- Other things

FROM UNMOTIVATED
TO INSPIRED

"When you do things from your soul,
you feel a river moving in you, a joy."

—*Rumi*

When we were at the beach one day, we watched an ugly thing happen. A father had taken his young sons and their friends (altogether four boys) for a day of surfing. The day was winding down, and everyone was removing their wet suits and packing up their gear in the car. Then the boys started arguing over who was going to sit next to whom. Suddenly, the dad exploded and yelled in a loud voice, "You (expletive!) kids! Shut your (expletive!) mouths! I'm sick and tired of hearing your (expletive!) arguing!" His language went on like this for several minutes. The boys, he said, were "stupid," "idiots," and he was "sick and tired of them." The tirade was so abusive that we were about to intervene, when, thankfully, the man stopped. The boys slunk silently into their seats, and they drove off.

What could have been a great day for those boys with their dad at the beach ended badly because he let himself stress out over what looked to us like harmless boyish behavior. In the "space between stimulus and response," this father had chosen to strike a hard blow at his relationship with his sons. The stress response can have harsh consequences. How will the boys feel about their father tomorrow? Next year? Many years from now? What effect will his example have on the behavior of his sons? Will they also learn to respond to stress by lashing out and driving the stress cycle through the roof?

Habit 2 in Stephen R. Covey's book is "Begin with the End in Mind." He writes, "To begin with the end in mind means to start with a clear understanding of your destination. It means to know where you're going so that you better understand where you are now and so that the steps you take are always in the right direction."[41]

If the angry dad had deliberately planned to destroy his relationship with his sons and to teach them to respond to stress with purple-faced rage, he could not have done a better job carrying out his plan. If that was the end he had in mind, he was certainly well on his way to achieving it.

Somehow, we doubt that was his overall plan for his family.

It's more likely that he had no plan, no overall mission in his mind for himself as a father. Maybe he'd never thought about it. Without a long-term plan, a goal, a vision in mind for the kind of father he wanted to be, he would continue to react stressfully to stimuli of the moment. Stress expert Roger T. Williams says, "No amount of relaxation techniques can overcome the stress created by an aimless life. Without direction, without purpose, without a reason for being, one's life becomes random, scattered, hit-and-miss."[42]

As Dr. Covey taught, people drift in a sea of uncertainty unless they discover their *mission*—the vision they have for their lives or their reason for living. He urged people to take the time to think through what they really want in life and to put it in writing. Suppose the dad had written a mission statement like this:

My mission as a father is to raise honorable and respectable children. They will be friends to all. They will act with generosity and kindness. And I want them to think of me as their best and most dependable friend, as one who loves them.

Now, this doesn't have to be everybody's mission statement; every parent will have his or her own mission in mind. But suppose he had written such a statement and committed himself to live by it. Suppose he revisited this statement regularly and often to recommit himself to it. The statement would become a guide to how he should act in the space between stimulus and response. In a moment of anger, he could think through "his end in mind": boys who are honorable, respectable, friendly, kind, and generous. If any response to his kids' actions had to run through this filter in his mental space, his response would be very different from the display we saw on the beach. He would have decided long before how to respond to stress instead of mindlessly reacting to it.

Sam writes:

As a young person, I ran everywhere. I was full of what people used to call "nervous energy"; today they call it "generalized anxiety," and they medicate you for it. Running was my way of handling a very stressful home life. My family members abused drugs, alcohol, and each other, including me. So I ran everywhere—to my friends' houses, to the 7-Eleven store, to school.

I also excelled at sports, primarily football and track because of all the running. I could go to football practice and knock people down and get rewarded for it—a great way for me to take out my frustrations and anxieties. On the track team I ran the 880- and the 440-yard events. I was big, so I could throw the shot and the discus better than anyone on our team, and I was very proud of that. I worked hard to get into that position.

One day after school, my stepbrother drove up in his mustard-yellow 1977 Gremlin, picked me up, and took me to an abandoned construction site. You didn't say no to him, you just sort of did what he told you to, and there he gave me drugs—a lot of drugs. Afterward I went home, went to bed, and just slept for two days. My parents didn't notice or didn't care.

Actually, no one noticed or cared. But I remember getting up and going to track practice in a dirt field behind the junior high school. I stretched and ran a warm-up lap. About halfway through that lap, I felt a crushing pain in my chest, and I collapsed in the dirt heaving for breath.

Then I had this amazing epiphany while lying there in the dirt. Somehow, some way, I suddenly knew that if I kept doing what my family was doing that I would end up just like them, living a miserable life. And I didn't want to be like them.

But I also knew in my heart that I could change. I didn't know how to change, but I knew I could. Deep in my core I knew I could create a different destiny. And that day on that track at Woodbury Junior High, in the dirt, I decided on my "end in mind." The freedom to choose our lives runs deeper than we really know.

Consider for a moment your own "end." Suppose you were an unseen spectator at your own funeral. Here comes a lifelong friend to deliver a eulogy. Then your boss says a few words. Now we will hear from your children. Last of all, your spouse or partner pays tribute to you.

What would you like each of these speakers to say about you and your life? What kind of partner, coworker, or parent would you like them to describe? What kind of son or daughter or relative? What kind of friend? As Dr. Covey asks, "What character would you like them to have seen in you? What achievements and contributions— to your friends, to your family, to your community—would you want them to remember? Look carefully at the people around you. What difference would you like to have made in their lives?"[43]

As you answer these questions, you will begin to detect your mission in life. Write down the answers. Keep them and revisit them regularly and often. If you do this, your mission statement will reduce your stress levels. Because so much stress is caused by uncertainty, just having a mission statement provides you with the inspiration you need to stay motivated. The pressures of the workplace are "stressful without sense," in the words of author David Whyte, unless we can make sense of them by having a clear "end in mind." What inspiring contribution do you want to make in your current role at work?[44]

Most stressed-out people have no sense of mission. They have trouble getting up in the morning because they're not motivated by what they're going to do that day. They have no inspiring end in mind, or if they once had it, they've lost sight of it in the day-to-day grind.

The unmotivated paradigm is when a person cannot or will not even attempt to deal with the constant stress, the pressure, the burnout, and the strains at home. But the inspired paradigm is when a person says, "I've got something really worthwhile to work for. I know the contribution I want to make. I can visualize the legacy I want to leave."

A lack of motivation is both a cause and a result of stress. If you're not motivated by your work, if it isn't compelling for you,

you will be stressed out. Then the resulting stress makes you even less motivated. "Nothing saps a person's motivation more than stress and worry . . . The biggest impact stress has on you professionally is that it causes your motivation to lag."[45]

The antidote is inspiration. You won't get negatively stressed out by work that inspires and excites you (although you may experience positive stress, as you might when competing in a game you love). With the Habit 2 paradigm, you have an "end in mind" that inspires and motivates you. Because you are deeply committed to your vision, you don't experience the hopelessness so many stressed-out people experience. If you revisit that mission statement regularly and often, it will become a "filter" in the space between stimulus and response.

WORKOUT: CREATING A MISSION STATEMENT

The purpose of this workout is to help you discover your primary mission and purpose in life, rather than living a stressful, aimless life.

What matters most to you in life? What is most important to you, and what do you value the most? What value, idea, or principle has such great worth that you would dedicate your life to be able to live by that principle?

Think back to the funeral scenario. Take a moment to write down all the values that came to mind. Do not list them in any order, but simply write down all of those values that seem to be worthwhile to you.

Next, consider each of the values you wrote, and rank them according to their worth to you. As you are doing this, you may want to consider the following question: "If I were to really design my own life, if I were going to create a set of values that shape the ultimate destiny I desire, what would they need to be and in what order?"

Finally, write a clarifying paragraph for each of your values. Answer the question: "What does this value really mean to me?" If you were living that value perfectly, what would your behavior be like, and how would you describe it?

Consider the following guidelines as you write each clarifying statement:

- Write each statement as an affirmation, a *positive statement*.
- Write each clarifying statement as an *"I" statement*.
- Write your clarifying paragraph in the *present tense* as if it were currently happening.

For example, a clarifying paragraph for the value of good health might sound like this:

I am healthy and strong. My body and mind function well at all times. I treat myself with respect. I eat well; I get plenty of exercise, sufficient rest, and manage my stress in excellent ways.

Once you have completed this process, you will have created your own personal mission to use as the standard for everything you do in your life.

As you live by your mission statement, you will start putting every decision you make, no matter how small, through that filter. Your deepest values will start to color all your choices, and your stress will lift.

How to apply that filter? Consider the choices you make during the day, and ask yourself, "Which choice will help me achieve my mission? Which action is most in accord with my values and principles?"

Once when we were teaching a group of prisoners, we asked them what they would do if a prison guard pushed them around. Most of them just shrugged, but one agitated prisoner said, "Knife him." After we taught them about the space between stimulus and response and the importance of "beginning with the end in mind," he changed his answer. "I wouldn't knife him." "Why not?" we asked. "Because it wouldn't help me achieve my mission to get out of here."

"Well," we thought, "that's a start." He now had a filter in the space between stimulus and response.

Avoiding stress is often just a matter of making that kind of decision. What's your end in mind? What do you want to have happen?

But what do you actually do in the space between stimulus and response? Here are some options to try:

Observe. Simply observe the situation. Don't say anything, and don't make judgments. It doesn't affect your mission.

Allow. Say to yourself, "I can live with this; I can go with the flow on this; it doesn't interfere very much with my mission."

Accept. Say to yourself, "I'm okay with this; this will help me achieve my mission."

Discover. Ask yourself, "What can I learn from this situation that will help me achieve my mission?"

Be grateful. Say to yourself, "I appreciate this experience. It's rich and rewarding."

An excited schoolboy rushed home on his motorbike to get something for a party he was invited to. He left the motorbike engine running while he ran inside. His father, arriving home from work, parked his car right behind the bike. In a hurry, the son backed out into his father's car, which he had failed to notice, causing significant damage.

If you were the boy's father, what would you say? "That was a really stupid thing to do"? Or "You're not going anywhere ever again on that motorbike"? Or "I'm sick and tired of your irresponsible behavior"?

You may have already chosen to be upset because of the damage, but do you think your stress level would rise or fall with those responses? What impact would those responses have on your son? Would you be alienating your son?

On the other hand, suppose you had a different end in mind— to teach your son responsibility while affirming your love and respect for him. "Thankfully, no one was hurt" (gratitude). "I have insurance to cover the damage, and I'm going to tone down my frustration" (allowance). "Well, I know you didn't intend to do this (allowance), but we're going to have to talk about the right way to drive a motorbike." You might even say to yourself, "I should have noticed that his motor was running and anticipated that he might be backing out soon" (discovery).

Each of these responses is driven by the father's mission—to maintain a strong relationship with his son. Instead of reacting impulsively, the father chooses his responses carefully, based on the higher mission he has set for himself.

You can do this. First, determine what's really important to you—what is your mission? What's the end you have in mind in your roles as a worker, a parent, a friend, a spouse—in short, for your whole life? Then start making small decisions based on that *big* decision. You will soon find that you have eliminated many of the stressors in your life.

If you want to unwind, decide *now* to "begin with the end in mind." Do this Inspiration Workout to make it happen.

WORKOUT: INSPIRATION

The purpose of this workout is to help you gain (or regain) the inspiration you need to overcome stress.

Earlier we asked: "How often in the last month have you felt unmotivated to 'get up and get going'?"

If you answered "fairly often" or "very often," you are experiencing high amounts of stress in this area. The goal is to be able to say "almost never" or even "never."

Fill out a mission statement for each of the following areas of your life and refer back to them each day for at least two months. Ask yourself each day how you are doing in keeping true to your mission.

What is your mission in life when it comes to your

- career?
- friends?
- spouse/partner?
- parent?
- children?
- community?

FROM PRESSURES
TO PRIORITIES

Stress is an ignorant state.
It believes that everything is an emergency.
—Natalie Goldberg

I'm really unmotivated to work today. The fact that I've been sick for days and have just returned from a business trip to face a pile of to-dos definitely has something to do with it. Oh, and the fact that just as I was trying to get energized to start working this morning the Internet died didn't help much.

So here I am, unmotivated to work but needing desperately to start plowing through the to-do list. This isn't a time when I can throw caution to the wind, call it a bad day, and just chill out watching stupid TV (but how I wish!).[46]

This is a real slice of a stressed-out person's life: so overloaded with things to do that all she wants to do is escape. (Of course, she realizes that escape would only create more stress.)

A small amount of stress is probably okay. But in this case, what psychologists call her "total stress load" is way too high. Pile on too much, and anyone will stress out, with all the harsh consequences that come with it. We become less effective; our confidence shrinks; our health starts to suffer; and our motivation goes out the door.

Even though we know all this, overload is one of the most common causes of stress in today's world. People are trying to do more with less. It's common for one person to be saddled with the jobs two or more people used to do. Families are under huge pressure. Add the technology overload we live with, and it's no wonder so many are stressed out of their minds.

One popular coping mechanism is "multitasking." But scientists are now providing strong evidence that you can't multitask and do things well. In fact, trying to do several things at once produces mediocre performance on all of the tasks—and a lot of stress—because of the way our brains work.

At the Posner & Keele Laboratories for Cognitive Neuroscience at the University of Oregon, Professor Ed Vogel is doing groundbreaking work, or perhaps we should say, "mind mapping" work. He's figuring out what happens to our brains when we set a target to reach (say, losing weight or learning to speak Spanish). Do brains with specific goals in mind work better than brains without targets to reach? And how many goals or ordinary tasks can a person's brain attend to at once?

To answer these questions, Vogel is using a whole armada of high-tech equipment: an MRI-guided transcranial magnetic stimulation unit, an eye tracker, an electroencephalogram (EEG) recording unit that measures electrical brain activity, and a functional MRI scanner ten times stronger than anything ever used before. With these "gadgets," Vogel is able to see the human brain working, with exceptional detail.

And what does he see? Well, as you might expect, it's a complex picture. But let's see if we can make it simple: Suppose someone you'd really like to talk to told you her telephone number, but you didn't write it down at the time. How likely are you to remember it a day or two later—or even a few minutes later? If you can't recall it, it's because other, unrelated things entered your brain—a coworker stopped by to chat, a pop-up ad appeared on your screen, or a text message buzzed you. These things, irrelevant to the phone number you wanted to remember, overloaded your "working memory," that part of your brain that allows you to hold a number of things in mind at once. But the working memory is very limited—usually capable of handling only three or four things at a time.

Vogel compares your working memory capacity to an exclusive nightclub—a place lots of people want to get into but which, unfortunately, can handle only so many partiers at once. Of course, one way to solve the limited access problem is to build a bigger nightclub (or in other words to develop your ability to remember more things at once). But that's really hard for most people. The working memory has very strict limits.

A better way, Vogel says, is to hire a big, burly bouncer to keep some people out so that those already inside can have a good time. In other words, if you want to remember the important things (like the phone number of the person you wanted to call back), you have to keep the unimportant things from getting into your memory in the first place.

And that's where your mission and goals come in. Without your mission and goals, you can't tell what's important and what isn't.

It turns out that setting a goal for yourself (say, to lose 10 pounds—4.5 kilos—in the next three months) helps your brain know what unwanted stimulation to keep out. Once a goal is set, a part of the brain called the *globus pallidus* (in the basal ganglia) serves as a sort of attentional bouncer that helps you focus on your goal while screening out irrelevant temptations. According to Vogel, if you have established a goal to achieve, no matter the actual capacity of your working memory, you will find your brain working *for* you by screening out incoming "flak" that might distract you from reaching your goal. You will find that you can be more mindful of what you are doing.

If you vaguely want to lose weight but don't set a specific goal to achieve it, the brain won't screen the stimuli from the outside. That means you might pop those chocolates into your mouth without thinking about it.[47] Instead of losing weight, you just stress out about it.

Because the brain can focus mindfully on only one thing at a time, multitasking will just stress you out. On the other hand, if you *do* focus on one thing at a time, your chances of doing that one thing with excellence go way up. That's just a natural principle. How many really fine people do you know who are unbelievably stressed out because they are so overloaded? They either don't know how to say no or feel they can't. They have the paradigm that life is unrelieved pressure. Often, they actually become addicted to the pressure, and even though it's burning them out, they can't stop.

Maybe you're one of them.

The opposite of the paradigm of pressure is the paradigm of priorities. Another natural principle is this: Some things are just more important than others. Some things are really important; others aren't. The stress in your life will go way down if you will simply recognize that and start saying no to things that just aren't that important.

> **STRESSBUSTER**
> Too many things to do? Write down the two or three most important things you need to do today. Schedule them. Now forget or postpone the rest.

"Easy for you to say," we can hear you thinking. "The reason I'm overloaded is that I *have* to do all these things. On top of a full-time job, I'm going to school at night, and then there's laundry, and my boyfriend is always complaining I don't have time for him, and my mother loads guilt on me for not calling her more often . . ."

From Sam:

As a college football player, you soon learn that a game is one bewildering battle after another. Preparation is essential, but there are so many people doing so many things so fast—many of them unpredictable—that you can get overwhelmed in a split second. Today, everyone's life is like that. How did we learn to deal with the complexity?

We were taught that we had primary responsibilities and secondary responsibilities. Never sacrifice the primary for the secondary. My primary responsibility was to block the opposing linebacker, and his responsibility was to attack my quarterback. My job was to stop him. Of course, I could be doing a lot of other jobs—helping the center if he was about to get squashed, for example. But I could not get distracted by those secondary jobs.

If we didn't know what was primary and what was secondary, we'd get confused trying to do everything. And in football, if you hesitate for a split second about what job to do, you're burned.

An even higher priority was schoolwork. Above all, we were student athletes. Academics first, athletics second. I remember a young starting player with a great talent—everyone said he'd be a professional someday—who lost sight of that priority. Georgia Tech was a demanding school, and because he didn't put first things first, he had to leave. He could have had an amazing career, but he did not get his priorities straight.

Prioritizing means you have a lot less stress. Those priorities come from your value system. When there's no question about what comes first and what comes second in your life, you can say no to secondary priorities and avoid the anxiety that comes from being overwhelmed with the complexity of life.

We're not disputing that you have many roles to play and lots of important things to do. That does not, however, change the natural principle that some things are more important than others. The trick is to set priorities. The real question is a mindful one: "What are the few most important things I need to focus on now? What does not need my focus right now?"

That brings us back to Ed Vogel's research, which shows that focusing on a few priorities—or even one—is key to doing them well and reducing stress.

A century ago, heat from a car's engine often caused the fuel to overheat and turn into vapor, like boiling water that turns into steam. The steam couldn't move through the fuel line, so the fuel-starved engine died. This was called vapor lock, and it was very frustrating. Before the days of fuel-injected engines, drivers would have to stop and wait for everything to cool down before the car would start again.

You may be like that. Perhaps you have a hundred things you want to accomplish in a day or dozens of goals you want to complete in a year. Under those overheated circumstances, you are very likely to get vapor lock. Little will get done; nothing will get done well; and you won't be able to move forward. Taking on too many goals or tasks at once has been the undoing of many corporations, and they can be your undoing too.

The pressure paradigm tells us that everything is equally important. We have to take care of *all* of it. But a priorities paradigm says that some things are more important than others, and we should give priority to those things that will help us achieve our mission.

One of the most important concepts Stephen R. Covey taught the world was "Habit 3: Put First Things First." In the hustle and bustle of doing many little things, the big things in your life might be at risk.

A neighbor of ours likes to garden. On his day off he wakes up determined to get his garden cleaned or his fruit tree trimmed or his roses planted. But he *never* gets his projects done, and he continually stresses out over it. Why does he fail? Because on the way to his project of the day, he always happens to see something else that needs work. Maybe he notices some weeds growing by the pavement or a fencepost that needs a little paint. He stops to do a little weeding here, a little touching up there, and so on. Before he knows it, he has spent all his time on everything *but* his original goal. If he could learn to prioritize his actions, he could get the most important tasks done. Keeping his goal at the forefront of his mind would allow him to ignore side projects that aren't as pressing and stop stressing himself.

Setting priorities doesn't really take heavy mental discipline, but it does take planning. Doing things is not as valuable as doing things *with purpose.* We recommend that you take time every week—about thirty minutes—to think deeply about your mission in life, your most important goals, and the few priorities you should attend to that week. Without that kind of planning, without a conscious set of priorities, you will bounce stressfully from one task to another like a helpless ball on a billiard table.

A group of Israeli neurobiologists at the Weizmann Institute of Science measured brain activity in a group of volunteers. They showed the volunteers pictures of animals and other objects and then asked them to put the pictures into categories. For instance, when the volunteers saw a photo of a dog, they would point to the animal category; when they saw a photo of a bus, they would point to the non-animal category, and so forth.

Showing the photos in rapid-fire succession, the researchers discovered something very interesting: When the volunteers were busy with the categorizing tasks, the part of the brain (the prefrontal cortex) that handles judgment, decision-making, and introspection almost entirely shut down. In other words, when people are fully engaged in a practical project, there is no bandwidth left for deeper analytical thinking. Indeed, such people may not even be aware of their surroundings.

The implications of this study are both positive and negative: Losing yourself in your work may be evidence of full engagement in the task at hand—clearly a good thing. But if you're always on one task after another, never taking time to reflect on the value and meaning of the work, you end up like a robot—always working, never thinking.

This research becomes especially important if you realize that the prefrontal cortex where introspection occurs is the same part of your brain where planning and decision making take place. Therefore, if you are not careful, you could find yourself living a crazy busy life filled with all sorts of things to do, but a life with little or no fulfillment because you don't pause often enough to evaluate what you're doing and why you're doing it. Your focus is scattered; you are trying to do too much at once—and you will get vapor lock.

There are lots of good things to fill your schedule, but they may not all be the *best* things. As Dr. Covey said, "You have to decide what your highest priorities are and have the courage—pleasantly, smiling, nonapologetically—to say 'no' to other things. And the way you do that is by having a bigger 'yes' burning inside. The enemy of the 'best' is often the good."[48]

Can you make a promise to yourself to take thirty minutes each week and maybe ten minutes each day from now on to reflect on your life's purpose and to synchronize your daily actions with that ultimate purpose?

If you want to Unwind, decide *now* to "put first things first." Do this Priorities Workout each week to make it happen.

WORKOUT: WEEKLY PRIORITIES

The purpose of this workout is to help you prioritize those things that are truly important and stop the stress of having to do too much.

Earlier we asked, "How often in the last month have you felt unable to cope with all the things you had to do?"

If you answered "fairly often" or "very often," you are experiencing high amounts of stress in this area. The goal is to be able to say "almost never" or even "never."

Once a week, reread your mission statement and answer this question: "What are the two or three most important things I should do this week to fulfill my mission?" Write down those three things, and then insert those things into your schedule. These are your "must-dos" for the week. Everything else is secondary.

FROM HASSLE
TO HARMONY

Observe good faith and justice toward all.
Cultivate peace and harmony with all.
—*George Washington*

Often it's the people in our lives who are sources of stress for us.

"My boss hassles me constantly."

"That customer has been nagging me for weeks."

"I wish my mother would get off my case."

"My kids bug me to the point I just want to say, 'Hey, stay out as long as you want. We'll see you around sometime.'"

"Hassle" is an American word from about the World War II era, and it's possibly a combination of the words *hustle* and *harass*. A "hassle" is an annoying interchange with someone else, an argument that sometimes rises to the level of a fight. Hassles with other people are some of the most common sources of stress, to the point that the "daily hassle" has become a synonym for stress.

If you're being hassled at work to the point that you feel threatened or bullied, the person to talk to is your human resources manager. But most of the time, the daily hassles we all face are based on natural human competitiveness—turf wars, territoriality, ego issues, and plain old fear—fear of losing ground, losing out, losing face, losing a deal, losing a job, or just simply "losing." No one wants to be a "loser." One way to characterize stress in our society is the struggle people go through in order to "win."

In our society, winning is extremely important. Who gets the highest score is a big issue. Which one of us will end up with the plum job, the nicest home, the most expensive car, the best clothes, the most money, the most successful children, the most points on the field or the least points on the golf course?

Our fear of losing explains much of the stress we experience, but that fear is based on a faulty paradigm: that life is a hassle with winners and losers. In reality, there are very few arenas in life where competition has any meaning, such as a playing field or a courtroom or a race to win a business contract. But in most of the important fields of our lives, competition is meaningless. For example, as Dr. Covey used to say, "Who's winning in your marriage? It's a ridiculous question. If both people aren't winning both are losing."[49]

If you're working together on a project, do you really want your coworkers to "lose"? If you're haggling over a business deal, do you really want the other side to lose? What if they do? What will happen the next time you need to do business with them? If you're arguing with your parents, will you feel that much better if they lose the argument? What happens to your relationship when you make them feel like losers?

You'll find that your stress levels will rise. Forcing other people to lose might make them turn on you in the spirit of "fair play," and you might very well pay a price down the road. Worse, however, is the effect on you. By manipulating people into a losing position, you lose a bit of your humanity.

That's why Dr. Covey's "Habit 4: Think Win–win" is so important to reducing your stress levels. Helping others to win in life, while you also win, is much more satisfying than beating them.

It was a freezing day in December 1943 over Germany. World War II was at its height. Charles Brown, an American bomber pilot, looked into the eyes of the German fighter pilot on his wing. "It's a nightmare," he thought, and waited for death. His own plane was helpless, full of holes, shot through by enemy fire.

For his part, the German pilot, Franz Stigler, had suffered greatly at the hands of the Americans. Most of his fellow pilots were dead. An American had killed his older brother. When he saw the bomber flying low, he closed in for the kill.

When he locked eyes with the American, something happened to him. He eased his finger off the trigger. He nodded at Charles Brown and, signaling him to follow, escorted him over the North Sea and saluted him before returning to Germany.

Even in the midst of a terrible war, both men "won" that day. They survived the war, and fifty years later they met again. They sought each other out in their old age and became fast friends. Stigler was now retired from his prosperous business, and Charles had been an aid worker helping people around the globe. Because they had spared each other, both men had created tremendous legacies.

When asked how he felt about Brown, Stigler fought tears before he said, "I love you, Charlie."[50]

What does this story have to do with your stress problem?

It shows that everyone can win, even under the worst competitive conditions. You can prevent the stress that accompanies battling other people by adopting a win–win mindset. If you go into every situation determined that everyone will benefit, you can avoid "hassle" and get to harmony with just about anyone. And you also benefit by getting into harmony with yourself.

Sam reports on his experience with the win–win concept:

In American football, winning matters. In this most competitive of environments, the glory often goes to the most visible players—the amazing passer, the fastest runner, the talented outside linebacker who can "do anything"—pick up a fumble, make a key tackle, or sack the quarterback at a critical point of the game. People go crazy over the "winners." They know your number, they scream for you.

I was one of those outside linebackers, and I loved it. Some glory came with it. But the coaches knew about my shoulder injuries, which made me vulnerable in that position, and a day came when the coaches pulled me aside and said, "We have a talented younger player who can do this job better than you. We need you on the offensive line where you can make a greater contribution to the team, and this guy can do better at your position."

Well, this was a big blow to me. It wasn't fair, and I said so. Going to the offensive line would make me a less important player, I thought. I didn't want to change.

But the coaches said, "Do you want to play or do you want to sit on the bench?" The real question was, "Do you want to contribute the best you have or hold onto a position someone else can do better?"

So I learned the hard way about the satisfaction that can come with the win–win mentality. I spent the game in the middle of the action where it can be very rough. You break your fingers, you take a beating, you go through a lot of suffering so the team can win. No one in the stands really knows what you sacrifice for the team to succeed. I learned that winning as a team was far greater than getting individual glory—especially at someone else's expense. That's a character issue.

On most teams, there are always two or three players sitting on the bench close to the coach. They are talented and able, but the coach can't quite trust them to get the job done. They are not at the point of understanding win–win—that making a contribution to the ultimate goal is far greater than grabbing at individual glory. Strangely enough, I felt far less stressed out making my contribution to a team win than I did prancing around the edges waiting for my chance to look good—or sitting on the bench. The intensity of the challenge and meeting it together—pouring your best energies into the team's victory—you come out invigorated instead of wound up inside."

The paradigm of hassle is that life is a battle, and in every battle there's a winner and a loser. You've got to compete or die. But for a person with a paradigm of harmony, life is not a competition. Everyone can win. No one really has to lose in order for me to win.

How do you get to win–win?

The process is not always simple, but the concept is. You find out what constitutes a "win" for the other party. That might mean just asking, or it could mean heavy research if you're conducting a business deal. It's generally a good idea to get as specific as possible in finding out what "win" means for that other person; you might find that your concepts are not very far apart at all.

One of the most successful businesses in America in recent years, the retail giant Costco, is famous for its quality and variety of goods. Of course, many stores carry high-quality goods; so what has made Costco a nearly miraculous success story in that highly competitive retail world? One very simple practice is a big part of the story: a generous return policy. A customer can return most products with virtually no questions asked. This practice means that no customer need fear "losing out" by making a purchase at Costco.

You might think this is a "lose" for Costco. Customers bringing products back all the time? Is that any way to run a business?

Actually, because Costco trusts its customers to do the right thing, they are rewarded by loyal customers who wouldn't shop anywhere else. By keeping their customers, they win.

Additionally, Costco pays workers considerably more than they could make elsewhere in the retail industry. That practice has worried some Costco shareholders, but in the long run they too have been happy about it, as the company has yielded historic returns on investment. The CEO says, "We know that paying employees good wages makes good sense for business. Instead of minimizing wages, we know it's a lot more profitable in the long term to minimize employee turnover and maximize employee productivity, commitment and loyalty."[51] Costco is a remarkable example of win–win thinking in the business world—here's a company where everyone wins: the customer, the employee, and the shareholder.

The same principle is true in your individual life. Think about it—how can the people in your life win while you are winning too? And if you had the habit of helping others win, wouldn't that mean far less stress for you and for them?

Of course it would.

Some situations are abusive, and in those situations there can be no win for anyone. The best thing to do then is to walk away. Dr. Covey calls this approach "win–win or no deal."

But in nearly all interactions you have with other people, win–win is possible. If you want to unwind, decide *now* to "think win–win." Use this Win–Win Workout to make it happen.

WORKOUT: WIN–WIN

The purpose of this workout is to help you reduce stress in your relationships with others by making sure everyone "wins."

Earlier we asked, "In the last month, how often have you felt you were 'losing ground' in your life?" You may have answered "fairly often" or "very often," but our goal is to be able to say "almost never" or even "never."

When working with others, ask yourself, "What is my win in this situation?"

Then find out what is their win. Ask or do research.

FROM ANXIETY
TO EMPATHY

If you understand each other you will be kind to each other.
Knowing someone well never leads to hate
and almost always leads to love.

—*John Steinbeck*

Your coworker comes crying to you. She's just lost her job. She whispers to you how badly she's been treated, how unfair it all is. What will she do now? She's got a family to support.

You start to stress out too. You feel sad, angry, helpless. What can you do?

Then the phone rings. It's a complaining customer. "What kind of business are you people running? Why can't you get one thing right? What am I paying for here? I want my money back!"

And your stress level hits the ceiling.

It's just always been true. We stress each other out. Other people make us anxious.

Personalities clash, temperaments conflict. You can think win–win and do well when there's a disagreement—but what if the issues are deeper than just a difference of opinion? What if emotions are in conflict?

Social stress is complex. The workplace can be a very anxious environment, full of emotional turmoil we often don't know how to handle. Also, we worry about the problems of our friends, our parents, our children. Often the things that stress us the most involve those who are closest to us.

How do you deal with the stressful complexity of human relations?

By practicing empathy.

Empathy is a key principle of human relations. It is the paradigm of putting yourself into another's place and truly understanding what that person thinks and feels.

Empathy is totally different from sympathy, although they are often confused.

Empathy is understanding what others feel. Sympathy is feeling sorry for others and comforting them.

Empathy is understanding what others think. Sympathy is agreeing with what others think. So, for example, empathy is saying, "Losing your job is deeply painful. You feel rejected and unfairly treated. You're really worried about what's going to become of you and your family." Sympathy is saying, "I feel so bad you lost your job. They treated you so unfairly. I'm sure you'll find another job soon. You're too good a worker to stay unemployed long."

Unlike sympathy, empathy doesn't require you to agree with others. It doesn't require you to solve their problems. It doesn't require you to "fix their flaws." It does require you to listen intensely and respectfully and patiently, so they know there is at least one person who truly understands how they feel.

Empathy is totally mindful. It requires you to be present here and now, thus relieving you of the stress of thinking about the past and the future. You don't have to worry about what has happened in the past—that's all over anyway, and your focus now is on understanding where this person *is*, not where he or she *was*. You don't have to worry about what will happen as a result of this conversation because for now you're just listening and putting yourself into the other's mind and heart.

Empathy drains the stress out of a situation. It takes only one person (you) to listen empathically to another to have this effect. When you do this, you're practicing what Dr. Covey calls "Habit 5: Seek First to Understand, Then to Be Understood." Habit 5, he says, "involves a very deep shift in paradigm. We typically seek first to be understood. Most people do not listen with the intent to understand; they listen with the intent to reply. They're either speaking or preparing to speak. They're filtering everything through their own paradigms, reading their autobiography into other people's lives."[52]

This paradigm causes anxiety as you try to cope with the other person's issues: You feel somehow responsible to help them. Maybe relating your own experience to theirs will help: "Let me tell you what I did when I lost my job . . ." Maybe they need your advice: "Go back into the boss and tell her you're not going without a fight!" Maybe they want you to take over their problem: "Let me see if I can sort this out with the boss. She can't just fire you like that!" But all of these responses just add to your stress.

Some researchers believe that women in our culture may be more likely than men to absorb the stress of the people around them. "We [women] are raised to pay attention to the emotional needs of others and to take care of them, which makes us more vulnerable to their stress," says Dr. Martha Kitzrow, professor of psychology at the University of Idaho. "We want to be supportive, but we end up taking too much responsibility for their well-being."[53]

By contrast, the paradigm of empathy doesn't produce anxiety. It produces understanding, and that is usually what people need most.

How do you practice empathy?

Listen to your friend patiently. Don't interrupt her. Put out of your mind your own need to respond. You don't need to respond—to become "responsible." You are not responsible. Just try to feel what she feels and understand what she is saying. Try to *become* her just for a while.

STRESSBUSTER

The next time you have a conversation, get lost in the world of the person you are talking to. Don't say anything about yourself. Just listen to their interests, their agenda, their world. Forget trying to help or advise or throw in your own "two cents." You will be surprised by how much it reduces your stress to just listen to someone else.

Your empathy will have a transformative effect on her. You have become a sounding board, a reflector of her own thoughts and feelings, so she can begin to resolve them. Intriguingly, she might even begin to think with you about how to move forward, find a new job, and deal with the turmoil her job loss will cause. There will come a time when she might benefit from your advice, but not yet.

Listen to the angry customer patiently. Don't let him control your response. See whether you can really understand what he is thinking and feeling. Feed back to him what he is saying, so he can tell that you understand. To do this, you don't have to agree with him, sympathize with him, or submit to his demands. All you have to do at this point is to understand him. You will probably hear the stress drain out of the customer's voice as he realizes he's talking to someone who understands him. At length you'll be able to have a win–win discussion without all the emotional anxiety.

The anxiety paradigm makes us think we need to intervene, to solve a person's problems and "fix" the situation. This often makes us feel helpless. But an empathy paradigm helps us see that what we need to do is understand a person's thoughts and feelings. My job is simply to listen to them, not to fix anything.

People need empathy more than ever in the turbulent world we live in. To have someone who understands you—who really feels what you feel and gets what you're saying—is one of the greatest of gifts.

Unfortunately, empathy seems to be on the decline. Researchers have found that most people rate themselves as less empathic than the average person in the last century, with a particularly steep drop since the year 2000. This is possibly the result of an increase in social isolation. We are more likely to live alone and less likely to join groups than people from a generation ago.[54]

The result of a decline in empathy is an increase in social anxiety. This is ironic because technology has made connecting with other people easy and instantaneous. But the rise of social media has the paradoxical effect of discouraging personal contact with others. It may be that technology is partly responsible for the fact that people are "cocooning" more than ever. We no longer need to be face to face, or even voice to ear, to communicate.

Cocooning is the practice of retreating into your private space and avoiding personal contact with other people. We feel safer in our cocoons. We resent having to leave them. As we become used to this, the day comes when it's just too hard to face others.

Also, other people mean responsibility. It seems less stressful to take care of ourselves and let other people do the same, but cocooning can actually increase our stress over time. New research tells us that social isolation affects the brain by changing how certain hormones are produced. These changes cause increased anxiety and even aggression.[55]

111

As people get more isolated, their empathy "muscles" deteriorate. "They don't allow themselves opportunities to learn how to interact with others successfully," says Negar Khaefi, psychotherapist and anxiety specialist. "One of the most important lines of defense against social anxiety is learning to build empathy."

Sam has this to say on the subject of empathy:

> I had a lot of success in business and wanted to give something back to the community, so I volunteered as a mentor to young men who were in juvenile detention. Here were teenagers in rooms with bars and tiny windows, some of them locked up for years.
>
> At first I thought I'd just go in and tell them to shape up and snap out of it. I wanted them to see my success in life and figured they would want to emulate it. So I went in yapping, talking at them about success and turning over a new leaf and getting their lives together. And I made no impact at all. My glorious example and accumulated wisdom fell flat.
>
> Every parent knows how that feels. Everybody who is trying to influence others in any way knows it. There's nothing quite as stressful in life as dealing with other people, especially when they won't live up to your righteous expectations.
>
> I shared my frustration with my wife, who is much wiser than I am. She told me I would never succeed with those boys unless I got lost in their world and truly understood where they were coming from. She said, "Until you really understand someone, they can't understand *you*. They don't understand your motives. Until you can say you really understand, nothing will really change."
>
> So I got lost in their world. I shut up and listened. "What's going on with you?" I'd ask, and then just sit back while they

talked. "What happened to put you in here? What interests you? Tell me more about that."

Soon I understood exactly what my wife was telling me. Here I had been trying to be a mentor without understanding the people I was mentoring, trying to give them advice and opinions they didn't care to hear. I had assumed they would automatically trust me, when all they saw was "Mr. Successful Businessman" trying to make himself feel good by condescending to visit them and share his "wisdom" with them. I learned that these young men had been betrayed their whole lives and didn't trust anyone.

One hard case was José. He was 18 and about to be released after five years in detention. He was so hardened, he would have killed anyone from a rival gang without a moment's thought. I learned that by listening to him. But instead of being outraged at his callousness, I just continued to listen with as much empathy as I could.

After a year and a half of just listening, I began to sense that José was starting to trust me and wanted to hear what I had to say in return. He knew I understood him. One day he looked at me as if a light had switched on in his head. "Sam, you're right. I don't have to kill or hurt people from other gangs. I can avoid these people." After his release, he went to community college and never returned to prison.

From a stressful and pointless activity, my time at the detention center turned into absolute pure joy.

Just resolving to listen without trying to fix their problems was a big stressbuster for me. I try to do the same with my family and my coworkers. Learning to listen with empathy is one of the best things I've done in my entire life, for my own sanity and for the sanity of other people. Only after you really understand someone, do you earn *the right* to share insight or teach the person anything."

You might feel stressed out in public or have a hard time connecting with other people. Habits of defensiveness have isolated you from others. As one researcher puts it, "You are turned inward . . . Too much of your mind space is devoted to keeping yourself safe."

"Empathy is the opposite of being turned inward. It is the ability to see another for who he or she is, and feeling what they might be feeling. This is an important skill to develop if you suffer from social anxiety because it is the first point of true connection with someone else . . . If you let yourself empathize for a moment with someone else, you may find that your anxiety begins to subside." As you understand more about the other person, you will see them as less threatening. "Understanding anything is the key to stop fearing it, and this concept also applies to other people."[56]

If you want to unwind, decide *now* to "seek first to understand." Use this Empathy Workout to make it happen.

WORKOUT: EMPATHY

The purpose of this workout is to help you reduce stress by increasing your understanding of others.

Earlier we asked, "In the last month, how often have you felt that other people were making you anxious?" You may have answered "fairly often" or "very often," but our goal is to feel this "almost never" or even "never."

Spend thirty to forty-five minutes listening empathically to someone who wants to talk, preferably about something that involves some emotional energy. Simply listen to him or her without any other agenda except to hear and understand. Focus all of your energy on listening for the single purpose of understanding. After you have finished, write down your answers to the following questions.

- Who was involved? What was the main topic of conversation?
- Describe as exactly as you can what the other person was saying. Explain what he or she was thinking and feeling.
- Describe how you noticed yourself vacillating between listening empathically and listening autobiographically (listening to your own thinking).
- Describe how the person you were talking with responded to you when you listened empathically.

FROM DEFENSIVE TO DIVERSE

He who is different from me does not impoverish me—he enriches me.

—Antoine de St. Exupery

Our world is an angry place. People shout at each other at the office. The media is cynical. Politicians seem more interested in one-upping each other than in working on real problems. People on the street are suspicious. Few fully trust the government, the corporate world, or any of the institutions that hold our society together. *Forbes* Magazine says 82 percent of workers don't trust their leaders to be honest with them.[57] Of course all of this adds to our collective and individual stress.

In such a world, the brain's built-in stress response comes into play, and we get angry. Anger is a natural response to a threat. If a poisonous snake strikes at you, you might erupt with anger and strike back at it. In a situation where you really are threatened, anger might even save you. But chronic anger can ruin your health. As Dr. Covey said, "Chasing after the poisonous snake that bites us will only drive the poison through our entire system. It is far better to take measures immediately to get the poison out."[58]

When someone disagrees with you or argues with you or just presents an idea different from yours, you might feel defensive. It can take the form of mild resentment or rise to the level of a shouting match; in either case, to some degree your competence is questioned, your position is at risk, your identity is challenged. A common reaction is to suppress your anger and withdraw.

Because it is so obvious a cause of stress, the paradigm of defensiveness has been studied for a long time. Researchers know that chronic defensiveness correlates dangerously with high blood pressure and heart disease. They also know that defensiveness is one of the main factors in what they call "job strain"—the stress you feel at work.[59]

The well-known educator Joshua Freedman, an expert on emotional intelligence, points out that when we become defensive and withdraw, "we feel vulnerable, stress kicks in, and we become less creative and collaborative. This reaction could make us more isolated and overwhelmed, which pushes us toward more stress."[60] It's natural to want to defend your territory, just as primitive people did for millennia. But constantly patrolling the borders of your self-image is highly stressful.

Actually, it's worse than stressful. By defending yourself automatically against ideas that differ from yours, you deny yourself the benefit of expanding your understanding. Everyone has a different perspective, and most great companies, families, or teams arise out of mixing up diverse people with diverse strengths and perspectives. As Freedman points out, we become less creative and collaborative because we can't work together with people of differing opinions. "If two people have the same opinion," Dr. Covey taught, "one of them is unnecessary."[61]

The world is full of proof that differences produce strength and sameness produces weakness. Many organizations suffer from "group think," commitment to a single point of view—usually the point of view of some powerful person—because group members are afraid to think for themselves. The group becomes defensive and vulnerable to disruption. "We didn't see it coming," is the usual response of executives blindsided by a new and dangerous idea from outside the tight circle of sameness.

Stress at home is often the result of defensiveness over differences. Too many marriages break up over petty differences that spiral out of control. Too many relationships between parents and children are poisoned by criticism, hostility, and cynical arguments. Professor Clayton Christensen of Harvard Business School, and also a graduate, writes, "A shocking number of my classmates, when they graduated from the Harvard Business School, every one of them planned to have a marriage that was just filled with joy and happiness. And a shocking number of them went out and got divorced two or three times. They find their children are being raised by someone they've never met on the other side of the country. And their family situation is a source of real pain. Not a single one of my classmates had a strategy to go out and get divorced and be unhappy."[62]

Defensiveness is a typical reason for family stress. A spouse makes a remark; the other spouse immediately becomes defensive. "You're late." "Well, I have to work, you know." "Don't you think I have to work?" "Do you call that 'work'—staying home all day and doing whatever?" And it gets worse from there as the partners defend their territory. They argue, they quarrel, they fight. The result is distance, disunity, discouragement. Soon the defensive cycle becomes a vicious cycle. People who once fell in love with each other fall into a defensive paradigm that poisons everything.

The opposite of defensiveness is the "diversity paradigm," a mindset that welcomes diverse people, opinions, attitudes, and truths. The defensive paradigm fights these things off; the diversity paradigm celebrates them. The defensive paradigm points out differences and views them as a threat, whereas the paradigm of diversity says that differences should be welcomed, understood, and benefited from.

If you have the diversity paradigm, you won't stress out when facing a difference of opinion. Instead, you will say, "You have a different opinion. I need to understand it." That question by itself eliminates virtually all the stress in any interaction. And it's an honest question.

If you have the Habit 6 paradigm, you actually welcome diversity of people, opinions, and contributions. When people can capitalize on their differences instead of defending themselves, we get creative solutions to stressful problems. That's how synergy works: The combined strengths of two people always add up to more than their individual strengths by themselves.

STRESSBUSTER

Try the synergy challenge when you're stressed out about a problem. Get together with some people you trust, people with different backgrounds or opinions. Ask them to think with you:
- Brainstorm outrageous, fun ideas—anything goes.
- Get lost in other people's ideas.

Only one rule: The best idea wins, and everyone agrees to it. A man named Reed Hastings got tired of paying "late fees" to a giant video rental company called Blockbuster. He figured out a different way to do video rentals that was more convenient for customers and didn't saddle them with harsh fees. Hastings started his own company, Netflix, and offered it to Blockbuster. He thought there might be "synergy" between the two companies.

Blockbuster laughed at Hastings and denied that he had anything they weren't already doing. As Netflix continued to disrupt their business, Blockbuster became more and more defensive about it. Stress levels rose. They never said, "You've got something different—we need to understand it and leverage it." At last, Blockbuster went bankrupt and Netflix flourished.

The defensiveness spiral makes it harder and harder to solve problems creatively. Big problems, as Freedman says, "require our most creative thinking and abilities to build coalition . . . The ability to connect is the number one need—and we're losing it."[63]

When you think about it, creativity *requires* differences in thinking. If you put a group of diverse people together, you'll get divergent views. This could turn into a high-stress argument, or a high-performance creative team—it depends on your paradigm. Put a rocket scientist, a bug expert, and a medical doctor into a room and see what comes out—maybe a new way to shoot down mosquitoes that carry malaria! But if you put only doctors in the room, you'll get sameness. Put a farmer, an artist, and a chemist into a room, and you might get a cool new design for a nonpolluting urban garden. But if you put only farmers in the room, you'll likely not get any new ideas.

Sam had this experience:

At one time I was made vice president of marketing for one of the world's largest carpet and flooring manufacturers. This was a high-pressure job because we were constantly trying to come up with new ideas to stay competitive. I would lie awake at night wondering how to sell more carpet. What was distinctive about us? Why should customers answer my phone call when they were getting many phone calls from many other companies?

In this job, my big stressbuster was synergy. It meant finding the best thinking from lots of different sources. It meant paying attention to lots of divergent ideas. And it meant really understanding the wants and needs of our clients.

Our big customers were designers and architects of commercial buildings. Most designers were women, very bright and powerful women; and we did heavy research on them, on their profiles, their tastes, their interests. My job was not just to sell carpet to them, but to build an emotional connection with them.

We teamed with others in the company and came up with lots of ideas for connecting with these customers. One colleague, Bob, vice president of sales for our premium brands, threw out the phrase "'Breast Cancer." I was intrigued. What did breast cancer have to do with selling carpet?

It turned out that Bob had done some research about the women we dealt with. He had learned that professional women were often more susceptible to breast cancer,[64] and that many of them cared deeply about the issue.

So Bob and I went to Texas to meet with the Susan G. Komen Foundation, an organization dedicated to increasing awareness and eradicating breast cancer. We asked them how we could help and came up with a plan: We would donate to the Komen Foundation twenty-five cents for every yard of premium carpet purchased by our clients.

But that's not all. We recruited artists, composers, and writers to come up with ideas for increasing awareness of this devastating disease. We spent hours with these folks each week and became really good friends. They made music, painted pictures about cancer and its many phases, and all were profoundly grateful for the chance to synergize around the topic. Our company put together a package of songs and art prints and sent thousands of copies to our customers.

The response was overwhelming. The clients' idea of our brand changed completely. They inundated us with gratitude, orders poured in, and our business boomed. But even more important, as a result of our campaign several of our clients reported that they had detected early signs of breast cancer in themselves.

The program continued for several years, and we sold tens of millions of dollars' worth of carpet we probably would never have sold without it. It was a remarkable instance of synergy— we did good in the community, we sold more carpet for more money, and above all we raised awareness and funds for stopping this terrible disease.

Instead of lying awake at night wondering how to sell more carpet, I used the principle of synergy to diminish my stress levels and raise our creativity levels. We were excited—we were selling a lot more than just carpet.

Openness to the creative ideas of others is an amazing way to unwind. "One of the benefits of creativity is stress reduction," says Professor Mark A. Runco of the University of Georgia. "It seems that stress and creativity have a complicated relationship . . . Creative persons stand either above or outside the norm . . . dissimilar people are treated by the remainder of society as a threat to the search for sameness."[65]

It would be revolutionary if politicians were able to go up to each other and say, "You see things differently. I need to listen to you." The stressful conflicts that beleaguer our governments would turn into creative problem-solving sessions.

When you have a family problem, how would it be if you could ask your spouse or your mother or father or son or daughter, "Are you willing to look at solutions we haven't thought of yet?" The result would be far less tension, anger, and pain and a lot more synergy.

If you want to unwind, decide *now* to "synergize." Use this Synergy Workout to make it happen.

WORKOUT: GOING FOR SYNERGY

The purpose of this workout is to enable you to reduce stress by going for synergy with others.

Earlier we asked, "In the last month, how often have you felt defensive and/or angry?" If you answered "fairly often" or "very often," you are experiencing high amounts of stress in this area. The goal is to be able to say "almost never" or even "never."

Synergy reduces stress and increases creativity. To practice synergy, remember these guidelines:

1. When you are faced with a differing opinion or a comment intended to provoke you, say, "You see things differently. I need to listen to you."

2. Listen empathically. Don't judge, interrupt, or comment. Empty your mind of your defensive responses, your opinions, your story. Try to understand the other person's story.

3. Ask, "Are you willing to look for a solution that is better than either one of us has come up with?"

4. If the answer is yes (and it will almost always be yes), brainstorm with that person. Combine your best thinking to arrive at a solution you both like.

FROM TENSE
TO TRANQUIL

Tension is who you think you should be.
Relaxation is who you are.

—*Chinese Proverb*

If you do the things we've talked about in this book, your stress levels will go way down. But we can't guarantee that stress won't overtake you anyway. The world is not predictable. Disease, earthquakes, war, economic downturns, accidents, nutty bosses, spooky neighbors—none of this is in your control, and if it happens, you're likely to be stressed.

So in this chapter we give you the best thinking and skills on how to reduce stress when, despite your best efforts to prevent it, it happens anyway. The story of Sam Bracken illustrates how to deal with debilitating stress when it does hit.

Everything in Sam's world told him he was worthless. He was conceived in coercion rather than love, and he remembers always being hungry. He was dumped at an orphanage at age four. At age five, an older boy, laughing, doused his arm in lighter fluid and lit him on fire. When his mom returned for Sam and then married, the boy who had lit him on fire became his stepbrother—and

Sam was filled with fear. His new stepdad beat him and abused him; neighbor kids abused him too. His stepbrother used him as a human dartboard, and introduced him to booze and bongs. He got C's, D's, and F's at school. At age fifteen he was homeless because his mom kicked him out so she could hang out with a motorcycle gang.[66] If anyone had a right to be stressed out by life, Sam did.

As we've seen, Sam is today far from being a victim of chronic stress.

What happened? How did Sam overcome overwhelming anxiety to become the emotionally vigorous, vibrant, contributing individual he is today?

Sam was proactive about his life. At thirteen he decided he wanted to crawl out of the hole he was in. He didn't wait for it to happen. He worked hard at it.

He envisioned what he wanted his whole life to be like. He recorded his personal mission after deep reflection and introspection.

He developed a few long-term goals and then spent about fifteen minutes a day reviewing them. The reviews helped him focus—to put first things first every day.

Despite his best efforts, however, the worst was yet to come. His recollection follows:

When I turned 18, I accepted an offer to play football at the Georgia Institute of Technology, one of the top colleges in the USA. The football team had tremendous success in the past. In my first year I did well as a freshman, but in my second year I ran into trouble.

When spring football practice started, something was wrong. When I hit my opponents, I would suffer terrible pain in my shoulders. My shoulders started going completely out of socket, and I was in massive, massive pain. I had been wearing a broken set of shoulder pads—a disastrous mistake.

"Sam, I'm sorry to tell you this," said the team doctor, "but your shoulders have been permanently damaged, and I don't think you can play football again."

I was just totally devastated. My whole self-worth was connected to my performance on the football field. I pleaded with him, "There's got to be a way." I couldn't bear the thought of not playing football. The doctor said, "We can perform these radical surgeries and tighten everything down and put titanium screws in your shoulders, and you'll have a chance to come back." I thought about that for one minute and I said, "Yeah, let's just have the surgery."

I remember waking up from surgery, and my arm was immobilized, and there were tubes coming out of my shoulder, blood was everywhere, and I was throwing up because of the pain. *What did they do to me? Oh my gosh, what have I gotten myself into?* Weeks later I was still barely able to move my arm, but it was time to have surgery on the second shoulder. It was just as excruciating, just as painful. As a result of this, I lost a bunch of weight, all the muscles I'd built up over the years atrophied, and I was pathetic. For the first time in my life, I think, I fell deep into depression.

My college friends invited me to go with them to the beach during a school break. They were having a lot of fun, but I was still in severe pain. I was in absolute hell. I was in misery, complete misery. I looked at the ocean, and I saw the beautiful blue waves coming in and the water going out, and I felt like my hope for a better life had gone out to sea. I got more and more depressed and sad, and finally I got to this point where I said to myself, *My life sucks, and it can't possibly get any worse than it is right now.*

At that very moment, a flock of seagulls flew overhead and pooped all over me.

But there, on the sandy beach, I once again made a decision. It became a defining moment. I realized something really powerful. I realized that if I went around feeling sorry for myself, thinking about how bad my life was, that I was going to be pooped on for the rest of my life. I burned that realization into my head. I went back to Atlanta and started getting up at 4:30 every morning. I swam for an hour, then I ran all the stadium stairs at Bobby Dodd Stadium. That took me another hour. Before my roommates were getting out of bed, I'd already worked out for two hours. After class, I went to physical therapy and worked very hard to regain the strength and flexibility that I'd lost. At the end of three months, everything worked out and it was all wonderful, right? No.

At the end of three months, I was still having minimal gains. Hard work was not paying off. I was very, very discouraged. I went to my coach and sat down with him. "Coach, I

WHOLE PERSON

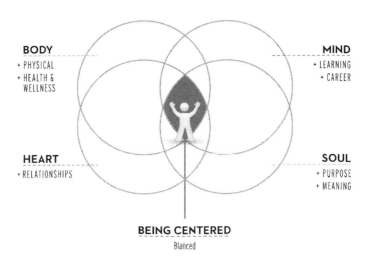

BODY
+ PHYSICAL
+ HEALTH &
  WELLNESS

MIND
+ LEARNING
+ CAREER

HEART
+ RELATIONSHIPS

SOUL
+ PURPOSE
+ MEANING

BEING CENTERED
Blanced

want to come back from these injuries so bad. I'm working really hard. I just don't know what to do." Fortunately, the coach saw me as more than just a football player. He saw me as a whole person. He listened very specifically to my concerns, and then he smiled and said, "Sam, I want you to do something for me. I want you to go to the bookstore, and I want you to get a 3-ring binder, and I want you to put four tabs in that 3-ring binder, and I want you to label them Mental, Physical, Emotional, Spiritual.

"Then I want you to put paper behind each tab, and I want you to write down where you are in each of those areas right now. Take a personal inventory of yourself. Take a hard look in the mirror. Write down where you are mentally, and write down where you are physically and spiritually and emotionally. Then, I want you to turn the page in each tab, and I want you to write down where you want to be a year from now. Be specific. Make sure your goals are narrow and that they're clear. And then, I want you turn the page in each tab and I want you to write down a compelling reason that you have the goal and how you're going to achieve it. I want you to read that book every day. I want you to positively obsess about where you're going and why you're going there and focus on how you're going to get there."

I did exactly what he said. I imagined what I wanted to be, and then I put down a few very powerful goals. I spent 15 or 20 minutes a day with this book, and it made all the difference. It helped me hold myself accountable to the change that I wanted. At the end of one year, every single thing I put in that book happened. Every single thing. Among other things, I raised my GPA, and I regained a starting position on a great football team."[67]

WORKOUT: SELF-TALK

The purpose of this workout is to help you change your "self-talk" so it is less negative and stress inducing.

Think of the mind as a recorder. We push the "Play" button and the same old thoughts that we had yesterday are played again today. Frequently, we play mental recordings that reflect thoughts of negativity, weakness, and low self-esteem. These recordings often include the constant repetition of many negative words, such as *no, can't, won't, maybe, never, if only I, I don't know, I ought to, I should, I need to*, and so on.

Bring to mind a situation or event in which your thoughts included some of these words about yourself. Write down your thoughts as they occur to you, without editing yourself to sound less stressed or more healthy.

Now, think of a different recording to listen to that would feed more positive messages into your subconscious mind. Consider using such positive words as these: "I am, I can, I will, I do."

How could you change your self-talk in the situation above so that you would act proactively instead of reactively? Peacefully instead of fearfully? Write down this new empowering recording.

Sam had worked hard at getting a handle on his life. Now he was confronting a serious injury that threatened his whole plan. How did he get through this most stressful time of his life?

He changed his paradigm. Instead of tensing up and obsessing over the disaster, he stepped back to look at his whole life in all its four dimensions: Mental, Physical, Emotional, Spiritual. He needed to take time to renew his mind, body, heart, and spirit.

The paradigm of tranquility is about keeping ourselves sharp in each of these dimensions. It means regularly and consistently renewing ourselves in wise and balanced ways. A carpenter who never stops sawing will soon have a dull saw. Likewise, people who are wound up too tight all the time will eventually wear out in exhaustion. For those with a paradigm of tension, the world is unremittingly stressful—just one mess after another—and the best they can do is try to survive. But a paradigm of tranquility says that the world is not inherently stressful, and one can choose to de-stress through "saw sharpening" activities in the mental, physical, emotional, and spiritual dimension.

You probably already do things to help you unwind in these four areas. If you have an exercise program, you may already know what we mean by "physical tranquility" due to the "high" or sense of euphoria that exercise produces in many people. When you're frazzled by a tough day, you might listen to your favorite music or read to calm your mind and spirit.

We've suggested below some exercises known to be potent de-stressors. You could call them "saw sharpeners" because they restore your energy when you're feeling stressed. You might want to try some or all of them.

Mental Tranquility Exercises

When you're in a stressful situation, try these mental tranquility exercises to turn off the stress response and calm your mind.

Guided Imagery. Some people call it visualization. It's the practice of imagining yourself in great detail in a place that relaxes your mind. Michael reports:

> In my class, I ask the students to close their eyes and imagine a big, ripe, juicy lemon on the table. I ask them to picture the lemon as clearly as possible, including its size, weight, texture,

smell. I then ask the students to take an imaginary but very sharp knife and cut the lemon into several pieces. Bring one section up to the nose, smell it, feel the juices leaking everywhere. Finally, I ask them to take a big bite of the lemon . . . and then another . . . and to imagine the juices of this sour lemon exploding as they chew. It's amazing to watch the sour contortions of their faces as they do this.

I then ask them how many have felt their mouths watering—usually about half of the class raise their hands.

This is the power of guided imagery.

When you find yourself stressed, find a comfortable place where you won't be disturbed. Then close your eyes and imagine something very pleasant. Picture it. Taste it. Smell it. Touch it. Engage as many senses as possible. Pretend you're in a quiet green forest or a mountain setting, or it's a warm, sunny day and you are walking on a beach. Imagine the smell of the ocean or the wildflowers. Imagine the light breeze touching your face. Imagine the warmth of the sand. You will find that your entire body calms down; your blood pressure drops; your heart rate slows; that twitch of your eye stops; and you start taking full, deep breaths instead of short, hurried ones. You'll have a few moments of serenity, some respite from the storms of your life. Both your body and your mind will be renewed, and you will better be able to think through and solve some of the issues causing you distress. Sam recollected his experience:

> As a young athlete, I was terribly afraid of failure. Here I was a member of a major college football team and scared to death that I would foul up on the playing field. Believe me, the thought of going up against a 6-foot 320-pound opponent who wanted to crush me in front of 80,000 people—that was stressful. What

was worse, I had to play with a lot of pain, immense pain. Even the thought of playing a game stressed me out.

I was lucky to have as a teacher Dr. Terry Maple, a psychologist who studied both human and animal behavior (he eventually became director of the Atlanta Zoo!). One day in class, Dr. Maple taught a lesson about the power of "visualization." I had never heard of this idea before.

So I asked him for some individual help, and he taught me how to visualize myself succeeding on the field. He explained the value of mentally creating my performance before actually doing it.

On this team we had one hundred twenty or so plays to memorize, each with eight different ways to execute, and every week the team planned in detail how we would approach the weekend game. With Dr. Maple's help, I would visualize the plan and play the games in my head before they even happened. I would darken my room, close my eyes, visualize a movie screen, and then picture myself going through each play.

Then one day I had to go into the game against Tennessee. Everything I had visualized that week happened that day, and in one game I moved from the third team to the first team. The coaches said, "Where did you come from, Bracken? How are you doing this?"

Visualization became an immensely powerful stressbuster for me. I became deeply confident because I knew in some detail what I would do before I had to do it.

Research on guided imagery has shown that it is effective in providing relief from chronic pain, headaches, and even asthma. It has also been shown to work on people with chemical dependencies and athletes suffering slumps in performance. It will work for you, especially if you use it regularly.

Relaxing Breathing. When your body's stress response kicks in, your breathing becomes quicker and shallower so you can get as much oxygen as possible to your limbs in case you need to flee or fight. In that case, your breathing is done primarily by the muscles in your shoulders and chest.

To unwind and calm the stress response, breathe differently. Start by closing your eyes. Then concentrate on how you breathe. Try to breathe from your stomach, not your chest. Take deep, slow breaths that cause your diaphragm to move down and your stomach to move out. Your chest doesn't need to move at all. Put your hands on your stomach so you can feel it move. Try pausing your breath for a moment between inhalation and exhalation.

If you find it difficult to fall asleep at night, try doing this breathing technique while thinking specifically of certain muscles you want to relax.

WORKOUT: BREATHING IN RHYTHM
WITH THE OCEAN

The purpose of this workout is to help you experience the relaxation that comes with deep, diaphragmatic breathing.

While lying down or sitting in a comfortable chair, close your eyes and picture, in your imagination, a beautiful sandy beach. Become aware of the ocean as its smooth waves flow in and out on the soft white sand.

Each time you slowly and deeply inhale, observe the gentle waves move toward you on the sand. As you exhale, see the gentle surf move back into the ocean.

As you imagine the in and out flowing of the waves in rhythm with your breath, sense the caressing waves as if they are washing over you, from your feet to the top of your head as you inhale, and the exhale washing down from the head back down to the toes.

Continue breathing slowly and deeply, and notice your breath, and the surf, moving slower and more effortlessly. While you are observing this, relax your jaw by separating your teeth and let your tongue relax more and more each time you exhale.

Continue breathing in and out with the gently flowing waves until you feel noticeably rested and relaxed.

When you are finished, very slowly return to your normal activities.

Mantra Meditation. During the day, your mind becomes agitated. There is a project due by 3:00 p.m.; there is an apology due as soon as possible for a misspoken comment in a meeting earlier in the day; there is a dental appointment. These and a million other things bind your brain, tie it up in knots, and clinch it so that it functions less effectively.

Meditation is a time-honored way to unwind. There is science behind it. Numerous studies indicate that during meditation the brain produces more alpha waves (electrical impulses that occur when we are relaxed or sleeping) and fewer beta waves (impulses that occur when we are highly stressed). As far as we know, meditation is one of the most powerful and effective ways to immediately turn off the stress response and place the body into a healing mode. So you might give it a try.

Find a place where you won't be disturbed. Sit in a chair (lying down usually doesn't work because you will likely fall asleep). Now, choose a word, any word, which you will repeat to yourself. Close your eyes and sit quietly for thirty seconds. Start saying the word slowly and softly in your head, at a pace of about one repetition every three or four seconds. Do this for about ten to twenty minutes.

If your mind wanders to other things, gently bring yourself back to repeating the word.

Then stop repeating the word, keep your eyes closed, and just remain seated for a minute or two to enjoy the serene feeling. Don't try to leave the peacefulness of the moment too quickly. Give yourself a full two to three minutes to return to waking consciousness. Do this once a day.

WORKOUT: HOW TO MEDITATE USING A MANTRA

The purpose of this workout is to help you learn how to meditate, and how meditation can reduce stress.

The most important thing is not to try too hard. Don't make a big deal out of this. It is the easiest thing that the mind can do . . . perhaps that is why it is so powerful.

1. Find a quiet environment where you won't be disturbed.
2. Sit comfortably *in a chair* (don't lie down) with your eyes closed. Try to be in a place with a minimum amount of noise and light, but don't be too concerned with noises. They need not be a distraction to meditation. People have meditated in airports, in the car, in boring classes or meetings, and many other places. The important thing is to go through the process as described below.
3. Begin by sitting for about thirty seconds with your eyes closed and just get yourself in tune with your internal environment. Do a quick scan of your body, observing how you currently feel from your head to your feet, but don't try to change anything, just notice what is happening as you passively observe.

4. Next, begin as effortlessly and silently as possible, repeating a word to yourself (not out loud). The word you choose is called a *mantra*.

   a. Examples of words (mantras) to use: *still, one, relax, peace, empty, calm, serene, silent, tranquil,* or any other word or phrase that is easy to remember. (It makes no difference what word you use. It only matters that you proceed with the simple intention of repeating the word over and over and over.)

   b. Simply repeat the mantra silently over and over to yourself, about once every four to five seconds.

   c. Just let your mind whisper your mantra under your thoughts, over and over and over. Don't try to change your thoughts in any way. Just allow yourself to keep whispering the word silently to yourself.

5. When you notice your mind wandering (it will), just notice it and gently bring your attention back to your mantra. Don't think that you are a bad meditator if you don't remain with your word the entire time or even part of the time. The important thing is to gently return to the word when you catch your mind wandering . . . or falling asleep.

6. Practice for approximately ten to twenty minutes every day (or at least three or four times per week). The best times to practice meditation are first thing in the morning and in the afternoon before the evening's activities. To enhance your experience, try a little yoga just before meditating.

7. Don't think that this has to be any more difficult than is explained here. There is nothing else to do besides silently repeat your mantra. Don't try to make anything happen.

Just be present with your mantra. That's all! You have only one intention while you meditate: Return to your mantra when it occurs to you to do so. There is no other effort involved whatsoever.

8. Sit with a clock in view if necessary. It is okay to briefly open your eyes to check the time, then close them again and return to the mantra.

9. When you are done, *slowly* return to normal waking consciousness. Take at least two minutes to return. Don't be in a hurry, or you might feel irritated, the same way you feel when an alarm clock or telephone awakens you out of a dream.

Several things might happen while you are meditating, and each is entirely appropriate.

• You might easily repeat the mantra for the entire period that you are meditating. This is fine but is not necessarily the goal. The goal is simply to repeat the word. Whether or not it happens easily is secondary.

• You might fall asleep. If you do, great. Enjoy it! You will probably have one of the deepest sleeps you have had in a while. Falling asleep while meditating is usually an indication that you need more sleep. You are giving yourself a perfect opportunity to catch up. When you do awaken from sleep while meditating, be sure to spend a few more minutes going back to the mantra. Then come out slowly for two or three minutes. Otherwise, you will feel like when you are dreaming and you are abruptly awakened to a phone ringing or some other very jarring sound.

• Another thing that might happen is your mind flying all over the place with thoughts. Don't be dismayed when this happens. Simply return to repeating the mantra. If your thoughts continue ceaselessly, just slip the mantra gently between your thoughts.

- Occasionally, though not very often, your mind will become very still. In that stillness, ideas, insights, inspiration, or intuition will flood into your mind. Be sure to have a pen and paper ready to write down the interesting thoughts that come to you. Out of that silence sometimes comes exactly what we need to know or do as we progress on our life's path.

Remember, the quality of a good meditation is not necessarily what happens during the meditation. The important issue is how you feel after meditating. If you have more energy, more alertness, if your mind is calmer, more peaceful, and you feel happier, this is feedback that your mind/body enjoys and finds benefit from the meditation.

Physical Tranquility Exercises

Physical tranquility comes from exercise and relaxation. In a state of stress, the body benefits from both.

Cardiovascular Exercise. We've learned about the stress response. "There's a snake!" The brain signals "fight or flee," and the entire body becomes chemically charged to do just that. Unless those signals are obeyed, the "fight or flee" chemicals continue to flow, maintaining the physiological imbalance.

Most people know the benefits of cardiovascular (CV) exercise—walking, running, swimming—to heart health. Exercise can also be a great stress reliever. The stressed-out body already wants to run—why not let it? It seems the logical thing to do, and it is. Exercise uses up the hormones adrenaline and cortisol that flood the bloodstream and every cell during the stress response. It also consumes the extra blood sugar and releases the increased muscle tension—thus satisfying the stress response and allowing you to go back to homeostasis. Essentially, if you've been telling yourself all day that you should be escaping some nonexistent threat, the smartest thing you can do is follow through on that message and run—or do whatever type of aerobic exercise you prefer.

What is the best cardiovascular exercise for managing stress? Simple—whatever exercises you will *do*! Find two or three types of exercise, and do them a few times a week. When you feel tense and agitated, go for a jog. You don't need to run 5 miles; don't overdo it, especially at first.

You might find other kinds of CV exercise that you like to do. Some people hate treadmills but love riding bicycles. Others enjoy Zumba, CrossFit, or tennis.

A good guideline for starting any exercise program is to determine what your maximum workout might be and begin at about half that level. For example, if you believe you can run 4 miles, run two as a baseline. Each time you jog, add just a little distance and intensity (sprint for a block or two or go at a slightly faster pace).

The worst thing you can do after a stressful day is to sit and fester in the stress hormones that are flowing through the body. You're stressed out—so flee! Run away from the snake for a while, and you'll be surprised by how relaxing it is and how good you feel.

WORKOUT: THE POWER OF EXERCISE TO REDUCE STRESS

The purpose of this workout is to help you see the benefits of cardiovascular exercise in reducing stress. Exercise, especially slightly higher intensity exercises like an aerobics class or playing basketball, satisfies the body's natural need to "fight or flee" by moving.

Exercise using any activity that will keep your heart rate elevated for thirty to sixty minutes. Do this activity at a time when you are feeling very high levels of stress, such as just before or after an important presentation or after you've been in a heated argument with someone. During this time of extreme stress, instead of watching TV, sitting and dwelling on the event, or grabbing a beer, move. Do something with enough intensity that you occasionally get out of breath and find yourself sweating.

After you are finished, notice the change in how you feel. The causes of your stress might not have changed, but you have fulfilled your body's need for a strenuous burst of energy to appease the "fight-or-flight" response. Now you can approach the situation in a more calm and levelheaded way.

Think through and perhaps write down your responses to these questions each time you do this workout:

1. Consider the situation in which you found yourself becoming stressed.
2. How did you feel before you started exercising? What stress-related symptoms were you experiencing?
3. What exercise or activity did you select?
4. Think about how you felt physically, emotionally, and mentally at the conclusion of your exercise session.

Yoga. The practice of yoga is thousands of years old. Most practitioners of yoga say it relieves their headaches and back pain and gives them a pervasive feeling of peace. Michael writes about his experience with yoga:

> I went to yoga instruction one day and was introduced to the teacher. She looked like she was about fifty-five, but she had the energy of someone in her early thirties. After she pushed us through an incredible 45-minute workout, a colleague told me she was well over eighty years old!

Yoga improves muscle strength, flexibility, and balance through a series of poses or postures. There are reportedly more than two thousand yoga poses, but most practitioners might do between twenty and twenty-five poses in an hour, sitting, kneeling, standing, lying on the back or the stomach, on hands and knees. The variations are almost limitless.

As a stress-reduction activity, yoga is very helpful. It relaxes the mind as well as the body. By focusing on breathing and holding the pose, you become mindful, you forget the stressors of the day, and you bring balance to your physiology.

Here are some suggestions for doing yoga.

- Find a class or a gym yoga group, or just do yoga at home to a TV yoga program.
- Hold poses for at least twenty seconds, although longer is better. The muscles, tendons, and ligaments need about that long to get into a stretching mode.
- Stretch until you feel you can't extend much further. Ease back a little from there. Then breathe and allow the stretch to increase just a tiny bit each time you exhale.
- Never push your stretch to the point of pain. You should feel a gentle pull on the muscles, but pain means you've gone too far.

- Go at your own pace. Don't compare yourself to anyone else. Body structures differ, and you're just fine at your own speed.
- Breathe deeply and slowly through the nose. As you hold a pose, keep the breath going freely and deeply. Never hold your breath while you are moving into or holding a pose.
- Practice yoga on an empty stomach. A full stomach inhibits your range of motion and saps your energy.
- Be present—listen to your body. Yoga is a great time to live in the moment and become aware of your body and what it can do.
- Enjoy the experience. This is a healthy thing to do, and the positive stress you undergo should be pleasurable.

If you're pressed for time, a helpful exercise from the world of kundalini yoga can help you. It's called *kirtan kriya*. You sit in a comfortable place for ten or twelve minutes and simply repeat a mantra. It should be a simple word, like *One*. Practitioners use the mantra *saa taa naa maa*, a series of sounds that calm the mind and soothe the nerves. Follow the same guidelines we mentioned earlier for mantra meditation when you do this relaxing exercise.

Relaxation Exercises

The opposite of the "fight-or-flight" stress response is the "relaxation response." Just as natural as the stress response, the relaxation response is the body's way of going back to homeostasis:

- Your breathing rate slows.
- Your blood pressure falls.
- Your heart rate slows.
- Your muscles relax.
- Your higher brain functions return to normal.

Notice that each of these effects is the exact opposite of the effects of acute stress.

You can activate the relaxation response through relaxation exercises. Just as when you lift weights to grow the size and strength of a muscle, relaxation exercises are designed to turn off the stress response by doing some simple techniques in specific ways. They are usually very easy to do. That's part of the reason why they are relaxing.

Here are some guidelines, as you practice relaxing:

- Seclude yourself where you will not be interrupted.
- Minimize background noises.
- Give yourself ten to twenty minutes each day practicing a relaxation activity, like breathing exercises or yoga or a power nap. Relaxation exercise is as important to your health and well-being as physical activity or a healthy diet.
- Try practicing the relaxation techniques at various times during the day. You'll find that, for you, some are more beneficial when you do them in the morning, whereas others seem to have a more positive effect in the afternoon or right before going to sleep.
- Do not be in any hurry to end the relaxation exercise. This is important. If you hurry to finish a relaxation exercise, it will feel like awaking from a deep sleep to a ringing telephone. It can leave you feeling off balance for the rest of the day. Take several minutes to return to normal waking consciousness.
- Turn off the telephone, the television, your mobile phone, and any devices with an alarm or any that may distract you.
- Approach each exercise without expectations: Be playful with the exercises. The best attitude to have when you do them is openness to whatever you experience. As you practice, say to

yourself, "I will take what I get. If I get nothing, then that is what I get—and that's okay. If I get some deep rest and relaxation, then that is what I get as well. It's also okay if I feel rejuvenated and energized." Trying too hard counteracts the desired effects.

- Regardless of how new or unusual any of these exercises might seem to you, they have been found to be effective in turning off the stress response and restoring balance. If you are resisting an exercise because it seems too unusual, simply thank that part of your mind for sharing its judgmental thoughts with you and continue in a playful, childlike way. Don't let the possibly strange nature of the method prevent you from experiencing it fully.

- The most important aspect of a relaxation exercise is not what happens during the exercise but how you feel *after completing it*. Don't judge a relaxation technique based on what happens during the exercise. You may not always feel relaxed while you are practicing. Your mind may feel like it is moving a million miles a minute. It doesn't matter. Relaxation exercises make you feel more balanced, alert, relaxed, refreshed, and energetic *the rest of the day*. If you do them right before falling asleep, they help you fall asleep much more quickly and get a better night's rest.

- Science cannot fully explain why some of these relaxation exercises work so well. With meditation, for example, science has not yet figured out why the simple repetition of a word produces such deep and profound rest. But it works.

Here is another more ambitious breathing exercise that can really relax and energize you for the rest of the day. We call it the *Power Nap*.

STRESSBUSTER

Try this quick but powerful relaxation exercise. While sitting or standing, slowly inhale through your nose. As you inhale, carefully move your shoulders up as high as you can toward your ears. Once they are as high as they can go, hold the breath and feel the tension. After a few moments of this, initiate a powerful releasing exhale, again through the nose, and as you do, release your shoulders back down very quickly and fairly forcefully. Notice the immediate difference between the tension and the relaxation you experience upon releasing your shoulders. Repeat as many times as you'd like.

Power Nap. Find a chair and lie down on the floor next to it, putting your legs on the seat of the chair. Stretch your arms above your head, and feel how this stretches your back too. Then slowly move your hands to your stomach so that you can monitor your breathing. Make sure you are taking deep breaths from your abdomen, not your chest. Consciously think of each set of muscles (your shoulders, your legs, etc.) becoming relaxed. Move your neck from side to side. Keep breathing and repeating these breathing movements for about ten minutes. Then take your feet off of the chair, and roll on your side in a fetal position for a moment or two. Slowly get up and go about your regular activities.

Progressive Relaxation. This exercise is usually done sitting or lying down. Begin the process by contracting or tensing up your feet. Consciously tense up the muscles—on a scale from 1 to 10, about a 7 or an 8. (Don't take it to the point where it becomes painful.)

  Hold the contraction and notice the sensation of tension as you hold it. Continue holding for about seven or eight seconds.

Then release the contraction. Consciously focus on your feet and notice the feeling of relaxation. Notice the difference between this and the tension that you felt before. Take a nice, full, deep breath and slowly exhale.

Now tense up the calves. You can flex these by pointing your toes as far away from you as possible. Hold this position for seven or eight seconds. Then, release the tension you have created, and focus on the feeling of relaxation in your calves. Take a deep full breath and exhale slowly. Continue this process in your thighs, your hips and buttocks, stomach, chest, lower back, upper back, neck, shoulders (push your shoulders up toward your ears), upper arms, lower arms and hands (make a fist), lower face (jaw, mouth, tongue), upper face (eyes, forehead, eyebrows), and finally tense the entire body at once. Hold it for about ten seconds. Relax it completely by inhaling fully and then exhaling slowly and effortlessly. At this point, you should be quite relaxed and at ease.

Short Naps. One of the simplest ways to unwind during the day is to take a brief nap. This type of nap, usually fifteen minutes or less, helps overcome grogginess and restore your alertness and energy. It's important not to nap for too long, or the body moves into the sleep cycle. If the full sleep cycle is interrupted, you'll wake up sleepy and disoriented. You might have a headache. But ten- to fifteen-minute naps are ideal for getting a quick recharge while preventing you from entering into the deep sleep cycle.

Sleep. One of the most important factors in dealing with stress is sleep. During sleep, your body turns on all of its healing energies to restore balance and heal the wounds of your day.

Most people get about an hour less sleep than they should be getting each night. That means, in a week's time, they've lost about a full night of sleep. This chronic lack of sleep can greatly contribute to stress.[68]

And even when they do sleep, they don't get deep, relaxing, restorative rest because they go to bed with the stress response still activated. As a result, the body expends its energy following through on the message to fight or run, rather than to rest, restore, and repair. So it's possible to awaken in the morning more tired than when we fell asleep. That's stressful!

Insufficient and poor quality sleep can result in these effects:

- Decrease your immune function
- Increase your risk for cancer
- Increase your risk for diabetes
- Interfere with growth hormone production
- Affect your ability to think clearly
- Increase the likelihood of several stress-related disorders, for example, heart disease; stomach ulcers; constipation; and mood disorders, including depression

With the stress response running, it can take a long time—thirty minutes, an hour, or even a couple hours—before sleep finally kicks in. While you're lying there trying so hard to fall asleep, your mind races with thoughts of everything that happened today and all the things you need to do tomorrow. When sleep doesn't come, you *try harder* to fall asleep. We know this just makes things worse.

Remember, your nervous system isn't aware of your body's location—in this case, in bed. It's only listening to your conscious thoughts. And if those thoughts involve *doing* things, you keep the body in a mode related to activity. These are not the kind of thoughts that the nervous system needs in order to shut things down for the day.

A baby, a child, or an adolescent typically falls asleep within about five minutes after lying down (if she's content). It shouldn't take much longer than that for you to fall asleep. And you shouldn't awaken during the middle of the night. If you do, you should be able to fall back to sleep pretty quickly.

If this isn't the way you sleep each night, there are things that you can do to help improve your sleeping patterns. The more of these you regularly do, the better sleep you'll get, both in quantity and quality. To improve your sleep, do these, on a regular basis:

- Exercise. Along with all of the other great reasons to exercise, aerobic activity helps pull you out of the stress response, utilizes the stress physiology, and creates the feel-good hormones we thrive on.
- Go to sleep earlier in the evening. Our ancestors did not enjoy the many modern conveniences that we do now with electricity, so for the most part they went to sleep when it got dark. Plenty of research indicates that our health will be better when we go to bed earlier rather than later.
- Remove from your diet all forms of caffeine and related substances (don't drink soft drinks). Caffeine is a stimulant, not a relaxant. By consuming caffeine, you keep your body geared up for activity. That's not going to help you fall asleep.
- Remove yourself from your electronic devices thirty minutes before falling asleep. You want to unwind prior to falling asleep. Frequently, the things we do with our electronic devices don't help us unwind.
- Don't eat within three to four hours before going to sleep. Nothing takes more energy (except exercise) than digestion. It's better to have your food fully digested when you need

to fall asleep so your energy isn't being drained working on your food.

- Keep your room as dark as possible while you sleep. Our ancestors did not sleep with lights on while they slept, and neither should we. If possible, block out all forms of light, turn off your nightlights, and close the doors to any other possible sources of light.
- Allow fresh, cool air into your room, if possible. It was natural for our ancestors to sleep in fresh night air; it's good for us too.
- Avoid sleep medication. Sleep medication might be a good idea on very rare occasions. The problem with sleep medications is their addictive nature. The more you use them, the more you need them. There is nothing natural or normal about trying to fall asleep with the aid of a chemical.

You get the most restorative rest when you practice sleeping according to the suggestions above. If you're having trouble falling asleep, try these actions:

- Do a mindfulness exercise. Focus as exclusively as possible on your breathing or your physiology or the things immediately around you.
- Vividly imagine your favorite place to relax—the beach, the mountains, a peaceful lake.
- Practice one of the guided imagery exercises mentioned in this book. Make sure it's the last thing you do before you close your eyes to fall asleep. And if you happen to fall asleep while you do one of the relaxation exercises, enjoy the deep sleep you've given yourself.

For more than twenty years I've been helping people manage their stress, and much of this work involves helping people improve their sleep. Over that time, nearly all of them have improved their sleeping experience by following these suggestions.

Nobody should have sleeping problems. Like headaches, they are unnecessary, they are bad for our health, and they are easy to fix—without chemicals.

Social/Emotional Tranquility Exercises

Social and emotional tranquility comes from nonstressful connections with other people. When you're giving service, on a date with friends, or just passing the time of day with somebody—in situations where "performance expectations" are low—you will find your stress levels dropping and your energy renewed.

Service. Helping others with *their* problems can reduce *your* stress. In fact, researchers have recently discovered that even those who have experienced a major stressful event can greatly lower their stress by helping others. Dr. Michael J. Poulin of the University of Buffalo said, "This study offers a significant contribution to our understanding of how giving assistance to others may offer health benefits to the giver by buffering the negative effects of stress."[69]

You don't have to do anything heroic; in fact, the study defined "service" as "the amount of time spent helping friends, neighbors, and family not living with them, by giving them gifts, doing their shopping, housework, running errands, and looking after children."[70]

Dr. Covey said, "There are so many ways to serve. Whether or not we belong to a church or service organization or have a job that provides meaningful service opportunities, not a day goes by that we can't at least serve one other human being by making deposits of unconditional love."[71]

It's not usually a great sacrifice to do these things, but the benefits in terms of stress reduction are significant. "While many of us feel too stressed and busy to worry about helping others with their burdens, or would like to think about doing good deeds when we have more 'spare' time, energy and money, altruism is its own reward, and can actually help you relieve stress."[72]

Connecting with Friends. According to Dr. Robert Sapolsky, "The single best predictor of an ability to deal well with stress is how socially connected you are."[73] Plan each week to connect deliberately with people who are important to you—relatives or friends. Don't let weeks slip by without making these connections, or they will weaken and disappear. Plan a party, a lunch or dinner out, a movie together—do something to keep the connection alive. You will find that a relaxing evening with friends improves your mood and lowers your stress levels.

Spiritual Tranquility Exercises

Spirituality is a broad area, including everything from religious worship and prayer to making a connection with nature. Whatever your idea of spiritual tranquility is, you should seek it in times of stress.

Inspirational Reading. In an English university study, a 68 percent drop in stress levels was gauged in people who simply sat down to read a good book—and after only six minutes! Heart rates dropped and muscle tension was eased.

The researchers believe the stress levels drop because the subjects have to concentrate on reading and the distraction eases muscular tension. "Losing yourself in a book is the ultimate relaxation," says Dr. David Lewis, who conducted the study. "You can escape from the worries and stresses of the everyday world . . . This is more than merely a distraction but an active engaging of the imagination."[74] We would say that reading is a very "mindful" experience.

The type of reading can make a difference as well. Reading popular novels that don't take much brainwork is a well-known way to unwind. On the other hand, literary classics that do engage your mind are beneficial too. Reading the "Great Books" like Greek philosophy or Victorian novels gives you a different kind of brain workout than day-to-day life requires. Dr. Kardaras says, "Certainly in a culture where most people's thoughts are focused on the empty preoccupations of shopping or video games or *American Idol*, a society where most people tend to be anxious and angry, there may be a need for the voices of the long-dead ancient Greek philosophers to come alive again to help us understand that what we think matters—that ideas and beauty and ethics and philosophy both *form* and *shape* us."[75]

Classical literature raises the questions that help us find meaning in life, which in turn reduces the stresses of lives that are too often lived automatically.

Listening to Music. People often mention listening to music as a favorite stress-reducer.

As leisure activities go, music is really relaxing because you don't have to watch or think about anything, as you would with books, movies, or games. David Lewis's study indicates that listening to music drops stress levels by 61 percent on average. Professor Nicholas Kardaras asks, "If you immerse yourself in playing a violent video game like *Grand Theft Auto* for hours a day instead of listening to classical music while engaging in informed discussions on the evolution of the universe for those same four hours, what might the impact be?"[76]

Research suggests that some types of music are better than others for reducing the stress response. Classical music with a slower tempo, particularly from the Baroque Period, seems to have the most relaxing effect. This period would include works by Bach, Haydn, Handel, Vivaldi, Telemann, and Pachelbel. Mozart also seems beneficial for reducing stress.

New Age instrumental music also has a relaxing effect. Its tendency to lack structure promotes a kind of "flowing" feeling in the listener, along with the generally quiet, somewhat rhythm-less character of the music. It can evoke flowing water, calm night sounds, or peaceful natural scenes. According to researcher Cynthia Ackrill, "Some music actually increases coherence of the heart rate—a really healthy state."

Benefits Finding. Because you can't predict tsunamis, earthquakes, or financial collapses, the best you might do is try to benefit from them rather than break down over them.

Strangely, people often report deriving real benefits from stressful events. These events are called "crucible" experiences, after the vessels in which ancient goldsmiths would melt gold to purify it. A crucible experience is a personal trial, often quite traumatic, that produces intense self-examination and change. Paradigms and priorities shift. People speak of what they learn from trials, such as patience, endurance, humility, and wisdom. For many, their family relations improve, their empathy increases, and they learn to keep their problems in perspective.

Psychologists call this "benefit finding." To reduce the stress of a hard time in your life, you can try finding the benefits you are gaining from the experience. What are you learning from your experience? What is changing in your paradigms? Are you becoming more empathic? More appreciative of the "little things" in life? More mindful? More aware of what really matters?

Intense stress can make you stronger, in the same way a muscle is strengthened only by stressing it. Dr. Covey tells this story:

I was in a gym one time with a friend of mine who has a PhD in exercise physiology. He was focusing on building strength. He asked me to "spot" him while he did some bench presses and told me at a certain point he'd ask me to take the weight. "But don't take it until I tell you," he said firmly.

So I watched and waited and prepared to take the weight. The weight went up and down, up and down. And I could see it begin to get harder. But he kept going. He would start to push it up and I'd think, "There's no way he's going to make it." But he'd make it. Then he'd slowly bring it back down and start back up again. Up and down, up and down.

Finally, as I looked at his face, straining with the effort, his blood vessels practically jumping out of his skin, I thought, "This is going to fall and collapse his chest. Maybe I should take the weight. Maybe he's lost control and he doesn't even know what he's doing." But he'd get it safely down. Then he'd start back up again. I couldn't believe it.

When he finally told me to take the weight, I said, "Why did you wait so long?"

"Almost all the benefit of the exercise comes at the very end, Stephen," he replied. "I'm trying to build strength. And that doesn't happen until the muscle fiber ruptures and the nerve fiber registers the pain. Then nature overcompensates and within 48 hours, the fiber is made stronger."

I could see his point. It's the same principle that works with emotional muscles as well, such as patience. When you exercise your patience beyond your past limits, the emotional fiber is broken, nature overcompensates, and next time the fiber is stronger.[77]

Crucible experiences can build your emotional fiber, making you more robust and resilient and, in the long run, less "stressable." That is an inescapable natural law. *The Economist* puts it well: "There are all sort of ways in which bad events contain useful information. Pain teaches children what to avoid. The failures of past entrepreneurs steer the next lot of start-ups away from the same mistakes."[78]

Benefit finding can reduce not only the emotional but also the physical symptoms of stress. There is some evidence that focusing on the benefits (rather than obsessing over the pain) can actually help the body get back to homeostasis.[79] Benefit finding correlates with lower depression, lower cortisol levels, faster recovery from illness, and an improved immune system.[80] People who find the benefits in tough jobs such as caring for the ill or the elderly are healthier on the average than those who don't like their work.[81]

Some months after a serious car accident in which his face was badly injured, author and professor Dave Logan observed, "Crucibles are the most demanding teachers of all, and their gifts are life-changing."[82]

J. K. Rowling became one of the most successful authors in history with her famous *Harry Potter* series. But before that, she had been poor, unknown, and depressed, even suicidal. She considered herself a complete failure. Now, in retrospect, she greatly values the things she learned "in the crucible." In her notable commencement speech at Harvard, "The Fringe Benefits of Failure," Rowling had this to say:

> Seven years after my graduation day, I had failed on an epic scale. An exceptionally short-lived marriage had imploded, and I was jobless, a lone parent, and as poor as it is possible to be in modern Britain without being homeless. By any usual standard, I was the biggest failure I knew.
>
> So why do I talk about the benefits of failure?
>
> Simply because failure meant a stripping away of the inessential. I stopped pretending to myself that I was anything other than what I was, and began to direct all my energy into finishing the only work that mattered to me. Had I really succeeded at anything else I might never have found the determination to succeed in the one arena where I believed I truly belonged. I was set free because my greatest fear had been realized, and I was still alive. I still had a daughter whom I adored. And I had an old typewriter and a big idea. So rock bottom became the solid foundation on which I rebuilt my life.[83]

Stressful life events can be our best teachers. If and when we have to go "into the crucible," perhaps the best thing we can do to calm the stress is to learn what it has to teach.

The "unwinding" exercises you've just learned about are only a few of the many de-stressors you could try. We suggest these because we know they work for many people. Some people like to go fishing or spend time in nature. Others like to get a massage or practice other forms of complementary and alternative therapies, such as aromatherapy or the Emotional Freedom Technique (EFT).

If you want to unwind, decide *now* to "unwind" deliberately in your life. Use this Unwinding Workout to make it happen.

WORKOUT: UNWINDING

The purpose of this workout is to reduce your stress levels by experimenting with the "unwinding" exercises you've been reading about.

Earlier we asked, "In the last month, how often have you felt stressed out because of something that happened unexpectedly?" If you answered "fairly often" or "very often," you are experiencing high amounts of stress in this area. The goal is to be able to say "almost never" or even "never."

Choose one or more of the suggested "stressbusters" to try in each of the four dimensions this week (or try one of your own choosing). Each day do at least one stressbuster for each of the four dimensions, and keep a small record of your progress.

- Mind: Guided Imagery, Mantra Meditation, Mindfulness
- Body: Cardiovascular Exercises, Breathing Exercises, Power Nap, Progressive Relaxation, Yoga
- Social/Emotional: Service, Connecting with Friends
- Spiritual: Inspiring Reading, Listening to Music, Benefit Finding

MAKE UNWINDING
A HABIT

Moral virtue comes about as a result of habit.
None of the moral virtues is engendered in us by
nature . . . their full development in us is due to habit.
—*Aristotle*

We've talked a lot about habits. People who have developed these stressbusting habits already know that our recipe for unwinding works. Some have found that, over a period of weeks, their breathing rate drops from thirty breaths per minute to as low as five or six per minute. Their blood pressure drops without medication. Their regular headaches no longer bother them. Some find tension and stress are things of the past. It becomes normal to fall asleep quickly, stay asleep, and awaken feeling fully refreshed. In essence, healing happens.

It doesn't happen overnight, however. You have to change your paradigms and apply them long enough that you expect to be calm. Just as you might now feel chronic stress is normal, you can come to expect peace and relaxation to be normal.

A friend of ours has been playing the piano since he was just four years old, even before he can remember doing it. Over the years, he has spent countless hours practicing the piano. Today, when he's playing a piece of music, his fingers automatically go to the notes indicated on the sheet music. He doesn't have to wonder where middle C or F-sharp is. He rarely has to look at the keyboard or his fingers. Playing notes and chords and patterns is so automatic to him that it is like blinking his eyes—he does it without thinking. Playing the piano is so "normal" to him that he wonders what it must be like for people who can't play.

You can make a stress-free life so normal that you won't be able to imagine living any other way. Your body wasn't designed for the maelstrom of chronic stress—its "true normal" is more tranquility than tension. But it won't happen until you change your habits.

We've already seen that it takes about sixty-six days on average to form a new habit. That's not really very long, just a little more than two months. Here's what to do.

Set an appointment with yourself once a week to go over your Workouts. It will take about an hour or less. Fill out each Workout each week and plan your week accordingly. If you'd like, include someone else in your planning—someone you can rely on for ideas and support.

Practice the new paradigms each day for two months. Practice makes normal—as you repeat an action, the brain rewires itself so that the action becomes easier each time you try it.

Set a goal to be less stressed two months from now. Envision where you want to be: "feeling peaceful," "no more headaches," "a day without depression," "getting to sleep more easily at night." A goal needs a measure of success, so select at least one. Measures might include your heart rate or breathing rate. You might want to track your stress levels against a makeshift scale: "Today I was at 10 on the Stress Scale—stressed out of my mind. Tomorrow, I'm trying for 9."

WORKOUT: THE "UNWINDING" CONTRACT

The purpose of this workout is to help you eliminate habits that are causing you stress and adopt habits that help you unwind.

You will more readily change the things in your life that produce stress if you make a written contract with yourself. We encourage you to make specific stress-reduction goals and commit to achieving them by a certain date. Here's how to create your "unwinding" contract:

Start by reviewing what you've read in this book and the activities you've tried. Consider all the relaxation exercises you have practiced and the insights you've gained as you read. Think through and perhaps write down your responses to the following questions:

1. What are the three most important things you have learned from this book and why? Give your answers careful thought and include your rationale for the relevance of this learning to your life.
2. What are your two most important stress management goals? Be specific about the outcomes you want by when.
3. You practiced various stress-reduction techniques as you read this book. What are the two that worked best for you, and why were they effective?
4. Consider what you will do to facilitate the accomplishment of your goals. Consider using the stress-reduction techniques that worked best for you.

5. What payoffs will you realize by fulfilling your goals?
6. Now choose a partner or coach to help you unwind. Select someone you trust and whose input you value, who will listen to you with an open mind and be honest in providing feedback. Share with that person the three most important things that you learned from this book. Include your major stressors, your reasons for wanting to manage stress better, and your plans for doing so. Ask for their perspective on both your stressors and your plan. After you have talked with this person, write your response to the following questions:

   • Whom did you talk to and why?
   • What input, advice, and observations did this person offer? What, if any, of this person's feedback was useful to you?
   • What did you learn from this sharing?

7. Now complete the following contract.
8. Don't forget to go back and retake the Stress Quiz on page 59 to gauge your progress.

Unwind Contract

I, _____, agree to enhance my health and quality of life by committing myself to the following goals for the next _____ weeks. This agreement with myself will be in effect from _____ to _____. At that time I will reassess my goals.

The two specific stress-management goals I have set for myself are (remember to make your goals specific and measurable, for example, "run 1 mile in ten minutes by December 1):

Goal 1:

Goal 2:

I realize I may sabotage my plans by:

So I will avoid this by:

Family members and friends who will assist me in reaching my goals:

The payoffs I will realize by fulfilling my goals:

My reward for keeping this contract:

Signed: _____

Witness: _____

Date: _____

ENDNOTES

1 Henry David Thoreau, *Walden: A Fully Annotated Edition*, Yale University Press, 2004, 72.

2 Judy Martin, "Stress at Work Is Bunk for Business," *Forbes*, August 2, 2012, http://www.forbes.com/sites/work-in-progress /2012/08/02/stress-at-work-is-bunk-for-business/.

3 K. Belkic, P. A. Landsbergis, P. L. Schnall, and D. Baker, "Is Job Strain a Major Source of Cardiovascular Disease Risk?" *Scandinavian Journal of Work, Environment, and Health*, 30(2), 2004:85–128.

4 "Work Organization and Stress-Related Disorders," NIOSH Program Portfolio, CDC, n.d., http://www.cdc.gov/niosh /programs/workorg/risks.html.

5 James W. Pennebaker, *Opening Up: The Healing Power of Expressing Emotions*, Guilford Press, 1997, 64.

6 "Well-Being—Absenteeism, Presentism, Costs and Challenges," *Occupational Medicine*, 58(8):522–524.

7 Bruce A. Cryer, *Neutralizing Workplace Stress: The Physiology of Human Performance and Organizational Effectiveness, presented at Psychological Disabilities in the Workplace*, The Centre for Professional Learning, Toronto, CA, June 12, 1996.

8 Research on Work-Related Stress, European Agency for Safety and Health at Work, Office for Official Publications, 2000, 29.

9   "Is Your Job Taking a Toll on Your Health?" *Times of India*, January 22, 2013, http://articles.timesofindia.indiatimes.com /2013-01-22/health/35934309_1_arm-pain-aches-forearms -neck-and-shoulders.

10 "'Heart Risk' to Career Women," *Mail Online*, n.d., http:// www.dailymail.co.uk/health/article-133084/Heart-risk-career -women.html.

11 "NIOSH Report on Stress," Just Breathe: A Wellness Sanctuary, December 5, 2006, http://www.justbreathewellness.com /justbreathe/index.php?s=fela.

12 A. Perkins, "Saving Money by Reducing Stress," *Harvard Business Review*, 72(6):12.

13 Benjamin Fearnow, "Study: 70 Percent of Americans on Prescription Drugs," *CBS News*, June 19, 2013, http://atlanta .cbslocal.com/2013/06/19/study-70-percent-of-americans-on -prescription-drugs-one-fifth-take-5-or-more/.

14 "Pan-European Study Confirms Link Between Work Stress and Heart Disease," UCL News, September 14, 2012, http://www .ucl.ac.uk/news/news-articles/1209/14092012-Stress-heart -disease-Kivimaki.

15 *Stress in America: Our Health at Risk*, American Psychological Association, January 11, 2012, 18, http://www.apa.org/news /press/releases/stress/2011/final-2011.pdf.

16 M. Kat Anderson and Jennifer House, "California's Ancient Cornucopia," The Weston A. Price Foundation, December 10, 2012, http://www.westonaprice.org/notes-from-yesteryear /californias-ancient-cornucopia; and "Resources for Teaching History in California," National Archives, n.d., http://www .archives.gov/pacific/education/curriculum, accessed May 6, 2013.

17 Exception: There is such a thing as "myocardial stunning," a dangerous heart condition brought about by sudden stress— such as the unexpected news of the death of a loved one or by

being "scared to death" when someone jumps out and surprises you. For more on this, see R. Bolli (Baylor College of Medicine, Texas), "Mechanism of Myocardial 'Stunning,'" *Circulation*, 82(3), September 1990:723–738.

18 Rika Morioka, "Anti-Karoshi Activism in a Corporate-Centered Society: Medical, Legal, and Housewife Activist Collaborations in Constructing Death from Overwork in Japan," eScholarship, University of California, 2008, http://www.escholarship .org/uc/item/98s1c756#page-1.

19 T. Hiyama and M, Yoshihara, "New Occupational Threats to Japanese Physicians: *Karoshi* (Death Due to Overwork) and *Karojisatsu* (Suicide Due to Overwork)," *Occupational and Environmental Medicine*, 65(6), June 2008:428–429. See also "Man, 45, Died of Overwork, Japanese Labor Bureau Says, SFGate.com, July 10, 2008, http://www.sfgate.com /business/article/Man-45-died-of-overwork-Japanese-labor -bureau-3206060.php; and http://mdn.mainichi.jp/national /news/20080429p2a00m0na015000c.html.

20 Tamara Mitchell, "Stress: Part 1: The Physiology of Stress," working-well.org, n.d., http://www.working-well.org/articles /pdf/Stress1.pdf.

21 Maia Szalavitz, "The Science of Stage Fright: How Stress Causes 'Brain Freeze,'" *Time*, November 28, 2011, http://healthland .time.com/2011/11/28/the-science-of-stage-fright-how-stress- causes-brain-freeze/.

22 "Among the academic cream of American universities—Harvard, Yale, Princeton, MIT, and the University of Chicago—it is UChicago that can most convincingly claim to provide the most rigorous, intense learning experience," http://www.uniintheusa .com/usa-unis/midwest/100048/university-of-chicago.

23 As told to Dean Collinwood in a conversation in 1977.

24 Stephen R. Covey, *The 7 Habits of Highly Effective People*, New York: Free Press, 309–310.

25   Viktor Frankl, *Man's Search for Meaning*, Boston, MA: Beacon Press, 2006, n.p.

26   Cindy Krischer Goodman, "Stressed Out! 83% in Survey Say They Are at Work," *Miami Herald*, April 9, 2013, http://www.miamiherald.com/2013/04/09/3332702/stressed-out-83-in-survey-say.html; and Lisa Belkin, "HuffPost Survey Reveals Lack of Sleep as a Major Cause of Stress Among Americans," HuffingtonPost.com, May 10, 2013, http://www.huffingtonpost.com/2013/04/29/stress-survey-sleep_n_3156991.html.

27   "British Stress Levels Increase to 35 Percent, Study Says," ADP Industry News, January 2012, http://www.adp-es.co.uk/adp-news/adp-industry-news/january-2012/british-stress-levels-increase-to-35-per-cent--study-says.

28   Constantine von Hoffman, "Suicide Rate Jumps Amid European Financial Crisis," CBS News, Money Watch, April 5, 2012,   http://www.cbsnews.com/8301-505123_162-57409506/suicide-rate-jumps-amid-european-financial-crisis/.

29   Scott Hensley, "Suicide Rate Climbs for Middle-Aged Americans," NPR, Shots, May 2, 2013, http://www.npr.org/blogs/health/2013/05/02/180545035/suicide-rate-climbs-for-middle-aged-americans?utm_source=NPR&utm_medium=facebook&utm_campaign=20130502.

30   T. Nhat Hanh, *Peace Is Every Step: The Path of Mindfulness in Everyday Life*, New York: Bantam Books, 1991.

31   Ann Harding, "Can Mindfulness Curb Overeating?" CNN.com, CNN Health, January 10, 2012, http://www.cnn.com/2012/01/10/health/mindful-curb-overeating.

32   Alan Watts, *This Is It: And Other Essays on Zen and Spiritual Experience*, New York: First Vintage Books, 1958.

33   Jon Kabat-Zinn, *Full Catastrophe Living: Using the Wisdom of Your Body and Mind to Face Stress*, Guildford, UK: Delta, 1990.

34   Phillippa Lally, Cornelia H. M. van Jaarsveld, Henry W. W. Potts, and Jane Wardle, "How Are Habits Formed? Modelling Habit

Formation in the Real World," *European Journal of Social Psychology*, 40(6), October 2010:998–1009.

35 Darcia Narvaez, "Adults Out of Control: The Spread of Stress Reactivity," *Psychology Today*, March 25, 2012, http://www .psychologytoday.com/blog/moral-landscapes/201203/adults -out-control-the-spread-stress-reactivity.

36 Susan Folkman, ed., *Oxford Handbook of Stress, Health, and Coping*, New York: Oxford University Press, 2010, 39.

37 James Stevenson, "Comment," *New Yorker*, January 26, 1981, http://www.newyorker.com/archive/1981/01/26/1981_01_26 _025_TNY_CARDS_000335123.

38 Folkman, ed., *Oxford Handbook*, 337–338.

39 Covey, *7 Habits of Highly Effective People*, 32.

40 Christopher Panza and Adam Potthast, *Ethics for Dummies*, Hoboken, NJ: Wiley, http://www.dummies.com/how-to /content/ethics-for-dummies-cheat-sheet.html.

41 Covey, *7 Habits of Highly Effective People*, 98.

42 Roger T. Williams, "Creatively Coping with Stress," *Journal of Extension*, 18(3), May–June 1980:24–30, http://www.joe.org /joe/1980may/80-3-a4.pdf.

43 Covey, *7 Habits of Highly Effective People*, 97.

44 David Whyte, *The Heart Aroused*, New York: Doubleday, 1996, 142.

45 Warren C. Zabloudil, *Being a Go-to-Tech*, Boca Raton, FL: Universal Publishers, 2012, 76.

46 Nataly Kogan, "What to Do When You're Totally Unmotivated at Work," *Work + Money*, April 14, 2008, http://shine.yahoo .com/work-money/what-to-do-when-youre-totally-unmotivated -at-work-159371.html.

47 You can learn more about this powerful "goal effect" by reading Edward Awh and Edward K. Vogel, "The Bouncer in the Brain," *Nature Neuroscience*, 11(1), January 2008:5–6.

48 Covey, *7 Habits of Highly Effective People*, 156.

49　Covey, *7 Habits of Highly Effective People*, 208.

50　John Blake, "Two Enemies Discover a Higher Call in Battle," CNN.com, March 9, 2013, http://www.cnn.com/2013/03/09 /living/higher-call-military-chivalry.

51　"Costco's Profit Soars to $537 Million Just Days after CEO Endorses Minimum Wage Increase," Huffingtonpost.com, March 12, 2013, http://www.huffingtonpost.com/2013/03/12 /costco-profit_n_2859250.html.

52　Covey, *7 Habits of Highly Effective People*, 239.

53　Caroline Hwang, "Is Stress Contagious? The Health Risks of Secondhand Stress," *Ladies Home Journal*, July 2006, http:// www.lhj.com/health/stress/relaxation-techniques/is-stress -contagious-the-health-risks-of-secondhand-stress/?page=1.

54　Jamil Zaki, "What, Me Care? Young Are Less Empathetic," *Scientific American*, January 19, 2011, http://www.scientificamerican .com/article.cfm?id=what-me-care.

55　Rick Nauert, "Stress Effects from Social Isolation Explained," PsychCentral.com, November 15, 2007, http://psychcentral .com/news/2007/11/15/stress-effects-from-social-isolation -explained/1542.html.

56　Negar Khaefi, "The Importance of Empathy in Decreasing Social Anxiety," July 17, 2012, http://negarkhaefi.com/articles /the-importance-of-empathy-in-decreasing-social-anxiety.html.

57　Ty Kiisel, "82 Percent of People Don't Trust The Boss to Tell Them the Truth," *Forbes*, January 30, 2013, http://www.forbes .com/sites/tykiisel/2013/01/30/82-percent-of-people-dont -trust-the-boss-to-tell-the-truth/.

58　Covey, *7 Habits of Highly Effective People*, 91.

59　"The Cardiovascular Effects of Defensiveness," *The Job Stress Network*, n.d., http://www.workhealth.org/index.html.

60　Joshua Freedman, "Stress Is Killing Me! Time for Emotional intelligence," *Psychology Today*, April 12, 2013,

http://www.6seconds.org/2013/04/12/stress-health-emotional
-intelligence/.

61 Covey, *7 Habits of Highly Effective People*, 278.

62 Derek Anderson, "Clayton Christensen Talks Venture Capital, Crowd Funding, and How to Measure Your Life." *Tech Crunch*, April 6, 2013, http://techcrunch.com/2013/04/06/clayton -christensen-talks-venture-capital-crowd-funding-and-how-to -measure-your-life/.

63 Freedman, "Stress Is Killing Me!".

64 For example, Roger Dobson, "Professional Women More Susceptible to Breast Cancer," *The Independent*, June 9, 2013, http://www.independent.co.uk/life-style/health-and-families /health-news/professional-women-more-susceptible-to-breast -cancer-8651359.html.

65 Mark A. Runco, *Creativity: Theories and Themes*, Burlington, MA: Academic Press, 2010, 99, 128.

66 Sam Bracken, *My Orange Duffel Bag: A Journey to Radical Change*, Winnipeg, Manitoba, Canada: Operation Orange Media, 2010.

67 You can go to www.sambracken.com to hear Sam tell his own story.

68 See "How Much Sleep Do We Really Need?" National Sleep Foundation, http://www.sleepfoundation.org/article/how-sleep -works/how-much-sleep-do-we-really-need.

69 "Being Generous Can Give You More Than a Warm Glow," *Daily Mail Online*, February 5, 2013, http://www.dailymail.co.uk /news/article-2274142/Scientists-reveal-generosity-protects -health-helps-live-longer.html.

70 Elizabeth Narins, "Pay It Forward, Live Longer," *Prevention*, February 2013, http://www.prevention.com/mind-body/emotional -health/helping-others-reduces-stress.

71 Covey, *7 Habits of Highly Effective People*, 299.

72 Elizabeth Scott, "Benefits of Altruism," *Stress Management*, March 13, 2011, http://stress.about.com/od/lowstresslifestyle/a/altruism.htm.

73 Christie Nicholson, "The Strongest Predictor for Low Stress," *Scientific American*, December 25, 2010, http://www.scientificamerican.com/podcast/episode.cfm?id=the-strongest-predictor-for-low-str-10-12-25.

74 "Reading Can Help Reduce Stress," *The Telegraph*, March 30, 2009, http://www.telegraph.co.uk/health/healthnews/5070874/Reading-can-help-reduce-stress.html.

75 Nicholas Kardaras, *How Plato and Pythagoras Can Save Your Life*, New York: Conari Press, 2011, 230–231.

76 Kardaras, *How Plato and Pythagoras Can Save Your Life*, 230.

77 Covey, *7 Habits of Highly Effective People*, 290–291.

78 "Stress Best," *The Economist*, November 17, 2012, http://www.economist.com/news/books-and-arts/21566619-how-surprises-make-you-stronger-stress-best.

79 Julienne E. Bower, Carissa A. Low, Judith Tedlie Moskowitz, Saviz Sepah, and Elissa Epel, "Benefit Finding and Physical Health: Positive Psychological Changes and Enhanced Allostasis," *Social and Personality Psychology Compass*, 2(1), 2008:233–234; Julienne E Bower, Judith Tedlie Moskowitz, and Elissa Epel, "Is Benefit Finding Good for Your Health?" *Current Directions in Psychological Science*, December 2009, 337–341; and C. R. Snyder and Shane J. Lopez, eds., *Handbook of Positive Psychology*, New York: Oxford University Press, 2001, 584–587.

80 "Bower et al., "Is Benefit Finding Good for Your Health?" 337 341; V. Tran, Deborah J. Wiebe, Katherine T. Fortenberry, Jorie M. Butler, and Cynthia A. Berg, "Benefit Finding, Affective Reactions to Diabetes Stress, and Diabetes Management among Early Adolescents," *Health Psychology*, 30(2), March 2011, 212–219.

81 Paula Span, "Caregiving's Hidden Benefits," *New York Times*, October 12, 2011, http://newoldage.blogs.nytimes.com/2011/10/12/caregivings-hidden-benefits/?_r=0.

82 Dave Logan, "My Accident Aftermath and What You Can Learn From It," CultureSync.net, April 29, 2013, http://www.culturesync.net/accident-aftermath/.

83 J. K. Rowling, "The Fringe Benefits of Failure," Ted.com, June 2008, http://www.ted.com/talks/jk_rowling_the_fringe_benefits_of_failure.html.

ACKNOWLEDGMENTS

Many people contributed to this book. We are grateful to our wonderful families for their support and to our many colleagues—too many to name—who have contributed so richly of their time and expertise. In particular, we'd like to thank Annie Oswald, FranklinCovey's media publishing director, who shepherded this product into the marketplace, and Zach Kristensen, who managed the production of the book. We are also grateful to Dr. Dean Collinwood for his elegant insights and to Dr. Breck England for his help in writing the manuscript.

And lastly, a shout-out to our friends at Grand Harbor: to Natalie Fedewa for the title—brilliant; and to Mark Pereira, Gary Krebs, and Dan Byrne for their support and their brilliant work from start to finish.

ABOUT THE AUTHORS

 **Dr. Michael Olpin** is a full professor and the director of the Health Promotion Program at Weber State University. He has studied and researched the science of stress management for over thirty years. He received his PhD in health education from Southern Illinois University, with his dissertation focusing on the stress response in college students. He earned his MA in health promotion and his BA in organizational psychology from Brigham Young University. He has taught at several universities across the nation including West Virginia University, Virginia Tech, Concord University, Southern Illinois University, Brigham Young University, and Weber State University.

Dr. Olpin's teaching includes many areas of health and wellness, but his primary focus remains on stress management, mind/body health, peak performance, mental and emotional wellness, health research methods, and wellness coaching. He has presented papers and spoken at many conferences, workshops, and seminars around the country. In addition to these speaking engagements, he also consults with sports teams and athletes, individuals, and other community groups.

He is coauthor of *Stress Management for Life: A Research Based Experiential Approach*, a textbook used in colleges and universities around the world. He is also the founder and director of the Stress

Relief Center at Weber State University, where he conducts research and works with thousands of students, faculty, staff, and community members in helping them reduce their stress and reach peak performance. His website, StressManagementPlace.com focuses on stress management and wellness education. He has produced video, CDs, DVDs, MP3s, and other media featuring stress reduction and relaxation training. He has also written the stress management book entitled *The World Is Not a Stressful Place*.

Dr. Olpin enjoys athletics and participates in a variety of sports. He enjoys spending time with his wife, Shanyn, and their four children, Analise, Erica, Adam, and Benjamin. He loves playing with his kids and coaching them in various sports. In his free time, you will find him biking and trail running in the beautiful mountains of northern Utah, where his family currently resides.

Kevin Garrett

Sam Bracken, who chronicles his story in *My Orange Duffel Bag: A Journey to Radical Change*, was homeless at age fifteen. He managed to graduate eleventh out of seven hundred students from his Las Vegas high school and landed a full-ride football scholarship to the Georgia Institute of Technology. The title of his graphic mini-memoir comes from his experience of leaving for college and packing everything he owned into an orange duffel bag.

Sam was a Brian Piccolo award nominee for overcoming potentially career-ending injuries to re-earn a starting position on one of Georgia Tech's best football teams in history, under Coach Bill Curry. He also earned a spot on the All ACC Academic team for two years running. Sam graduated with honors in 1986, earning a degree in industrial management. In 1993 he received an MBA with a marketing emphasis from Brigham Young University's Marriott School of Management.

He and his wife, Kim, live in Kaysville, Utah, and have four children: Beau, Ben, Jacob, and Hannah. Sam serves as the a Managing Partner for Government Services at FranklinCovey, the world's leading training and leadership organization, with services in more than one hundred forty countries.

A member of the National Speakers Association, Sam frequently speaks about how to implement radical personal change. He serves as the national spokesperson for, and was co-founder of, the Orange Duffel Bag Foundation, a 501c3 nonprofit foundation that provides life plan coaching and training for at-risk youth ages twelve to twenty-four—especially focusing on youth aging out of foster care, as well as homeless teens. It is one of few organizations in the United States that offers professional level coaching to at-risk youth.

My Orange Duffel Bag has won eight national and international awards. Crown Archetype, a division of Random House, launched the book in 2012.

18622756R00114

Printed in Great Britain
by Amazon